JONATHAN EDWARDS:
A MINI·THEOLOGY

JONATHAN EDWARDS: A MINI-THEOLOGY

John H. Gerstner

Tyndale House Publishers, Inc. Wheaton, Illinois

Second printing, December 1987

Library of Congress Catalog Card Number 86-51381
ISBN 0-8423-1956-5
Copyright © 1987 by John H. Gerstner
Printed in the United States of America

To my very dear,
loving, and patient wife
for whom, along with our family,
Edwards
has become a household word
for some forty years,
to our eternal benefit.

CONTENTS

INTRODUCTION

The late Perry Miller, an influential interpreter of Puritanism, claimed that Jonathan Edwards' treatise *Freedom of the Will* alone was enough to establish him as the greatest philosopher-theologian ever to grace the American scene. If that is a sound evaluation, as we believe it to be, it is rather startling that there never has been a thorough study of Jonathan Edwards' theology. America's greatest theologian never produced — or had produced for him — a theology. Edwards himself did not produce one because he died before he completed his *Rational Account of the Main Doctrines of the Christian Religion Attempted* (usually referred to as the *Rational Account*).

Nor have any of his disciples who have written extensively about his theology ever put the picture together. Jan Ribberbos, in his *De Theologie van Jonathan Edwards*,[1] was entirely too general for any kind of adequate representation of Edwards' theology. On the other hand, Conrad Cherry's *Theology of Jonathan Edwards: A Reappraisal* is too specific to qualify as a theology of Edwards.[2] It is a useful, intensive study of one aspect of Edwards' theology. Carl Bogue's is more comprehensive than Cherry's, but it, too, focuses excellently on one particular doctrine, a very central one indeed: the covenant.[3] My own *Steps to Salvation* is more comprehensive, theologically speaking, than any other attempt, but it is restricted largely to sermonic material, leaves many major items untouched, and pays inadequate attention to secondary sources.[4]

This present work is a mini-theology. It has two reasons for existence. First, though brief, it nevertheless is based on the total corpus of Edwards' writings, with some attention given to secondary works, the large corpus of writings about Edwards. At the same time, it gives insights into twelve crucial theological affirmations of Edwards. For those who want an introduction and nothing more than an introduction to Edwards' theology, this book ought to serve that purpose. Second, this present work is meant to be a harbinger of things to come: a larger study of Edwards' theology. An exhausting attempt at exhaustiveness is in my heart, but whether it is in the decree of God remains to be seen.

Parts of this book have been presented at numerous theological seminaries during the last few years. Some of the 1975 Griffin-Thomas Lectures at Dallas Theological Seminary appear in chapter 2, as do parts of the 1980 Jubilee Lecture at Westminster Theological Seminary. The 1983 Spring Lectures at Western Baptist Seminary in Portland are scattered throughout, while fragments of the 1986 lectures on virtue at St. Louis's Covenant Theological Seminary appear in chapter 9.

My unbounded gratitude also goes out to the Yale University's Beinecke Rare Book and Manuscript Library with its excellent facilities and service provided by Marjorie Wynne and a most competent battery of associates.

Many Edwardsean scholars, living and dead, have by their writings and verbal comments contributed greatly to my understanding of Edwards. I mention particularly the outstanding researcher Thomas A. Schafer of McCormick Theological Seminary in Chicago. The Ligonier Ministries under the direction of R. C. Sproul, my very dear friend and fellow Edwardsean, Chris C. McCampbell, and Robert H. Love, together with many others, have contributed substantially to the expenses involved in my research, covering many years. My wife, Edna, and our son, Jonathan, have their life-blood in these pages.

That oft-quoted statement of Samuel Hopkins that one finds it very difficult to speak about Jonathan Edwards without seeming to be guilty of adulation certainly applies to this present writer. My indebtedness to the saint of Stockbridge is greater than to any other human being who has ever lived outside of the pages of Holy Scripture itself. Someone at an Evangelical Theological Society conference, listening to me lecture on Edwards, asked the question: "What faults do you detect in him?" That was about a minute and a half before the end of the hour. The audience broke out in laughter when the bell rang and I still had not responded to the question. I am afraid I am guilty somewhat of the adulation of Edwards that Jean Cadier of Montpelier, France, showed toward Calvin when he was asked whether he thought Calvin was infallible. He answered that he was sure Calvin was not infallible, but *he* could not detect an instance of his fallibility.

I am not quite that far gone on Edwards. I do recognize certain fallacies in Edwards, some of which will be discussed in this little volume. In my opinion, however, Edwards came closer to ascertaining the mind of God in the realm of rational reflection and biblical investigation than any other person. I hope that the reader will not become prejudiced *against* Edwards because he thinks the writer about Edwards is prejudiced *for* him. As Paul says, "We preach not ourselves," and not any other human being, but Christ only. By this standard only must Jonathan Edwards be judged.

Most readers will find, as I have, that Edwards measured his own life and thought against the standard of Christ. He did this at a critical time in the history of the church, a time when the rationalistic, man-centered thought of Enlightenment Europe threatened the orthodoxy of the American colonies. Judging Enlightenment thought by biblical standards, he found it severely lacking. But he had to meet it on its own terms, for he knew that the survival of pure Christian thought meant that creative, thinking Christians must rationally defend biblical orthodoxy against rising rationalism. He did this well, and brought Puritanism into a new age. That his life and work are still known and appreciated is evidence that his work was not in vain.

ONE

JONATHAN EDWARDS' PLACE IN THE HISTORY OF CHRISTIAN THOUGHT

Born in 1703 in East Windsor, Connecticut, Jonathan Edwards lived at a time when the Calvinistic Puritanism of the American colonies, particularly New England, was giving way to more man-centered thought coming out of Europe. Edwards held firmly to the theology of his Puritan heritage, yet he read with interest the philosophy coming out of Enlightenment Europe. He had both eyes on the biblical theology that had dominated the church for centuries — and both eyes on such new thinkers as John Locke and Isaac Newton.

There has been considerable debate over whether Edwards was the last of the medieval Scholastic theologians or the first of the modern American philosopher-theologians. The advocates of the former position point especially to his views of biblical authority, God and the Devil, heaven and hell. The latter are impressed with his development of Newtonian and Lockean thought, which was avant-garde in the 1700s.

Each of these views is correct. Jonathan Edwards was a rational, logical theologian of the medieval sort; he was also something of a Lockean idealist with Newtonian overtones. Vincent Tomas is quite right: Edwards "took orders" from the

13

Bible as truly and indeed more so than any Scholastic theologian of the Middle Ages.[1] But Perry Miller is also correct in noting that Edwards as a thinker was not only ahead of his time but also of our time, and was not only somewhat Lockean in his empirical approach but that he even extended Locke's ideas to homiletics, so that in this technical sense Edwards was a "sensationalistic" preacher.[2] On the other hand, Clarence H. Faust insists that even Edwards' scientific studies were but a subtle form of grinding his theological axe,[3] while Theodore Hornberger argues that Edwards employed the most modern philosophical means to save science from materialism, and that Edwards even used Newton's theory of atoms in the argument against Arminianism.[4] Douglas Elwood can see in Edwards a Neoplatonic panentheist,[5] while Robert C. Whittemore contends that the Neoplatonists were not panentheists and Edwards was simply a mystic.[6]

Each of these views is incorrect if considered mutually exclusive. The assumption that an orthodox theologian, devoted to the theology of the past, could not also gain insights from contemporary philosophy is based on a misconception of traditional Christian orthodoxy. Critics assume that orthodox Christianity is fideistic and nonrational. They also wrongly fancy that Lockean thought is "rationalistic" in such a sense as to exclude orthodox Christianity. John Locke (1632–1704) was, to be sure, the author of *The Reasonableness of Christianity*, but to make a rationalistic deist or Unitarian out of Locke because he thought of Christianity as rational only shows how little orthodoxy is understood. P. T. Forsyth wrote that the orthodox are more rational than the rationalists. The orthodox are not rationalists, but they can be rational.

Every evidence indicates that Jonathan Edwards was as orthodox in his view of reason as in everything else. It was no coincidence that his unfinished magnum opus was to be entitled *A Rational Account*. Even Douglas Elwood, who by no means does justice to the rational element in Edwardsean thought, grants in an understatement: "It must be admitted that there are places where Edwards sounds like any other eighteenth-century apologist."[7] The truth about Edwards is, as his son Jonathan boasted, he was more rational than most of his fellow Calvinists—that is, he tended to explain rationally what most other Reformed theologians were inclined to leave in mystery.[8] (It should be remembered that *mystery*, for the orthodox, was not the irrational but simply the partially understood; they always assumed that what was mysterious was capable of being understood, and someday, at least in heaven, would be.) Edwards believed in mystery too, and was quite content to await heaven for the complete and perfect explanation; but he was more inclined to go further in his explanations of mystery than were most other theologians. For example, the difference between him and Martin Luther in the matter of human freedom in relation to divine sovereignty was characteristic. Both believed the two doctrines, but Luther believed them though they appeared (to him) absurd and Edwards believed them while refuting charges of their absurdity.[9] In other words, Edwards felt that, using logic and the Bible, a man could reconcile the two doctrines and thus show that there was no absurdity at all. Edwards shared, with many secular philosophers of the Enlightenment, a faith in man's ability to reason properly and work out problems logically.

But Peter Gay, a specialist in the Enlightenment, thinks that Edwards had no place in that movement of the human mind. According to Gay, if a thinker were enlightened he was "rational," and if he were rational he would be "enlightened." Edwards was in a cage (his Puritan theological heritage) and not enlightened (in Gay's use of the term), and therefore he was not a son of the Enlightenment or a genuine disciple of

15

TOTAL DEPRAVITY
EFFECTS THIS
AS WELL

Locke. Locke (as seen by Gay), precisely because he believed in the "reasonableness" of Christianity, reduced it to a simple belief in Jesus as the Messiah and rejected all that was supernatural. Gay even gives the impression that the celebrated English empiricist had no place for miracles in his system of thought.[10]

How a reader of *The Reasonableness of Christianity* and other religious writings of Locke could maintain such a view is difficult to understand. Locke, to be sure, was indisposed to over-much mystery and liked clear definitions (as did René Descartes, who was Roman Catholic), but he believed far more than just the doctrine that Jesus was the Messiah, though he believed this was all that was essential to salvation. Furthermore, he regarded miracles as establishing the "credit of the proposer" of doctrine.[11] Locke was an orthodox Anglican, though he argued about some Anglican doctrines. The deists, who denied the reality of miracles and the divinity of Christ, were, unlike Locke, having their books burned and their very lives endangered. (Edwards reveals the status of deists in his own mind when, in an unpublished sermon preached in 1731, he refers to "robbers, pirates and deists" with apologies to the robbers and pirates.[12])

Locke's own intimate friend and disciple, Anthony Collins, moved from deism to an outright rejection of Christianity. But Locke himself never did. The doctrines he continued to affirm included the theistic proofs, miracles, the historic Adam, the historic Fall, the divinity of Christ, justification by faith, and many others. It is significant that Jonathan Edwards had not only read Locke's *Essay Concerning Human Understanding* but was also familiar with his *Paraphrase and Notes on the Epistles of St. Paul to the Galatians, Corinthians, Romans, and Ephesians*. Locke, like Isaac Newton, spent his latter days poring over the pages of the Bible, which he recognized as authoritative. Edwards' "taking orders" from

Scripture, therefore, does not prove him not to be a Lockean and a child of the Enlightenment in some of its aspects. Of course, if being "enlightened" must mean being unorthodox and/or unchristian, then Edwards must be denied that classification, along with Newton, Locke, Leibniz, the Cambridge Platonists, and many other thinkers past and present.

John Opie's *Jonathan Edwards and the Enlightenment* is a very useful little anthology, but it is odd that a volume on Edwards and the Enlightenment would fail to mention how Edwards actually dealt with the negative conclusions of the "enlightened" ones whom he knew as deists. In his unpublished "Miscellanies" Edwards addressed himself (especially in Miscellany 1340) directly to Matthew Tindal, deistic author of *Christianity as Old as the Creation, or the Gospel a Republication of the Religion of Nature* (1739) which is commonly called the "Bible of deism." Edwards went directly to the fundamental principle of deism, its rejection of Christianity and all revelation in the name of what it thought to be reason. Just as Edwards was later to show that the champions of free will reduced freedom to bondage and, worse than that, to meaninglessness, so he shows that deism, in its attempt to glorify reason, actually destroyed it.

The fundamental principle of deism—and the kind of "enlightenment" that Peter Gay has in mind—is that reason is not only the test of whether a revelation had been given but also of each item in that revelation. The orthodox Puritan Christian agreed that reason should be used to test whether a true revelation had been given, but once it was satisfied on that point, then reason (to be reasonable) would accept the content of that revelation without further testing. Reason, the Puritans felt, was never more reasonable than when it refused to argue about the things which were *above reason*. This sentiment characterized virtually all enlightened orthodox thinkers, Liebniz, Locke, and Newton included.

Edwards not only justified the enlightened character of the orthodox position, but proceeded to demonstrate the unreasonableness of the deistic stance. First, he pointed out that once we satisfy ourselves that sense perception, memory, and tradition are reliable, we accept their testimony without further ado.[13] If we did not, we could know virtually nothing. Edwards argued that all knowledge would be reduced to hopeless paradox if we could not rely upon the processes of perception and testimony. "That something now is," for example, is about the most basic piece of information we have, and yet that would be a totally baffling, nonsensical statement if we did not trust the testimony of sense and experience.[14] Rubbing this rationalistic point into proud deistic heads, he reminded them that the divine knowledge which they took for granted (including such beliefs as the immortality of the soul, a divine Creator, an orderly universe, a moral law) had been gotten from the revelation of Scripture. He observes that only where the Bible has gone has the knowledge of God prevailed.[15] In this connection he stresses the point (also made by Locke) that it is one thing to recognize truth when it is revealed and another to discover it apart from that.[16] Edwards ends his treatise with the statement that the deists, who were great proponents of education and schools, were inconsistent inasmuch as, in their view, knowledge is native to the human mind and man should not need to be taught knowledge.[17] We will examine Edwards' position on revelation and reason much more thoroughly in the following chapter.

Edwards maintains the common historic Christian viewpoint with unusual intellectual vigor. Many today misunderstand Edwards and Christianity precisely at this point. The historic Christian position has been, in spite of the prevailing contemporary notion to the contrary, a reason-plus-faith synthesis. Many today think that faith-minus-reason is the

Christian position because it is so common in our time. That, however, is a caricature of Christian belief. It is not the consensus of the church's tradition. But certainly reason-minus-faith, which may be a caricature even of rationalism, is not the consensus either. If one looks at the whole history of Christian thought, it is the reason-plus-faith synthesis of Edwards which emerges dominant.

TWO

REASON AND REVELATION

In the 1700s, philosophers of the Enlightenment claimed that reason was all man needed to live peacefully and morally. The orthodox Christians, Edwards among them, disagreed, since they saw that man needs the special revelation given to man in the Scriptures. Thoughtful Christians could not merely shove aside the claims of the rationalists, however. They had to explain the relationship between reason and revelation. Fine philosophical minds were needed for this task.

Never in history did a finer philosophical mind than that of Jonathan Edwards give its sustained and almost undivided lifetime attention to the Bible, examining it for its exegetical detail, historico-redemptive sweep, theological system, and above all its evangelistic use and effects. Edwards preached without ceasing (literally, vacations being unheard of). He commented on virtually every text (often entering the critical arena), and tied it all together (beginning with election and Adam and reaching via the Book of Revelation into his own time and beyond). He was eschatologically oriented always. Edwards worked the Bible into the greatest possession of orthodoxy, defended its fundamental doctrines by the deepest analysis of the human will ever produced, and examined its doctrine of religious affections definitively. And while he majored in God's book of special revelation, he did not neglect his book of nature, natural theology. He actually grounded the Bible in natural theology while vindicating natural theology by it.

THE HARMONY OF REASON AND REVELATION

Basic to any discussion of Edwards' view of revelation is his understanding of reason. Reason comes first in his thinking just as it does in his existence. Revelation is subsequent in thought as well as in being.[1]

While Edwards states in Miscellany 1337 that "the light of nature is in no sense whatsoever sufficient to discover this religion [Christianity]," he also writes that "there is perfect harmony" between reason and revelation.[2] This perfect harmony is not spelled out in any one work, but scattered indications are everywhere. He mentions often the role reason plays in supporting and fulfilling revelation. We may mention eight distinct functions of reason.

THE FUNCTIONS OF REASON

First, reason must prove the existence of God, the Revealer. Second, reason anticipates that there will be a revelation. Third, reason alone can grasp rationally any "pretended" revelation. Fourth, only reason can demonstrate the rationality of revelation. Fifth, reason must verify any revelation as genuine. (That is, it can discern when revelation really is revelation.) Sixth, reason argues revelation's dependability. Seventh, reason, having anticipated mysteries in any genuine divine revelation, defends them, refuting any objections to their presence. Eighth, though the "divine and supernatural light" does not come from reason, it is reason that comprehends what this light illumines.

Reason must prove the existence of God, the Revealer. It is clear that man's reason — even fallen reason — can and does prove the being of God independently of special revelation. We can never forget the words of Miscellany 1340, Edwards' most thorough demonstration of "the insufficiency of reason as a substitute for revelation." In this work he claims, "Nothing is more certain than that there must be an unmade and unlimited being." God is the Alpha and the Omega of the rational process. There is no thought that does not lead to God. Atheism is the ultimate absurdity. Every blade of grass gives overwhelming testimony to the divine being.[3]

In his sermon on the inspired Scriptures we read that "reason is to determine that there is a God, and that the Scripture is his Word."[4] This is seldom noticed in Edwards, his emphasis on reason being eclipsed by the greater stress which he places on revelation. For example, the 1 Corinthians 2:11-13 sermon so stresses the preaching of the "dictated" Word of God and not man's own wisdom that one barely notices the almost incidental reminder that man's own reason must first prove the dictated revelation to be from God. Likewise, all readers of the Matthew 16:17 sermon are so impressed with the necessity of the divine and supernatural light that they do not hear Edwards quietly observing, negatively, that this does not preclude the use of natural faculties such as reason.[5]

Reason must demonstrate the rationality of revelation. Edwards, for all his subtlety and penetration, is a typical eighteenth-century apologist. Indeed, he may even be called a typical nineteenth-century apologist. The nineteenth-century Princeton theologian Charles Hodge, for example, takes es-

sentially the same steps as Edwards in discussing the func-
tion of reason in revelation.[6] What Hodge calls the *usus or-
ganicus* (organic use) is our third point: Reason must grasp,
perceive, or understand what the purported revelation is saying, if anything.[7] Our present point is Hodge's view of reason as making trials or tests of contradiction *(judicium
contradictionis)*. Reason, having grasped the message, must
then determine whether it is coherent or believable—that is,
noncontradictory.[8] For the orthodox, who strive for rationality and consistency, contradiction is fatal to truth or even
meaning. It is the modern neo-orthodox theologians who
call for a "crucifixion of the intellect." Emil Brunner takes the
ultimate anti-orthodox position that contradiction is the
very test of religious truth: "The hallmark of logical inconsistency clings to all genuine pronouncements of faith."[9]

Edwards is orthodox, not neo-orthodox. For him, contradiction is the hallmark of nonsense. If consistency is, as
Emerson claims, the "hobgoblin of little minds," Jonathan
Edwards is the most small-minded philosopher-theologian
ever to mar the American scene. According to Edwards, it is
not wise but wicked men who are inconsistent with themselves.[10] This sermon on Matthew 11:16-19 is Edwards' man-
ifesto of a rational kingdom. Written in it is his counterpart
to Henry Dodwell's *Christianity Not Founded on Argument*
(1742).

Putting the whole matter more succinctly: The Bible
"shines bright with the amiable simplicity of truth."[11] Not
only is all that is found in Scripture true, but there are no
sound views maintained outside that are not derivative from
the Bible. Where the Scriptures have come there has been
light; all the rest of the world has remained in darkness: "So
'tis now all over the world," he told his little Indian congregation on the edge of the wilderness.

REASON, MIRACLES, AND REVELATION

Although Edwards nowhere uses Locke's expression "credentials of a messenger" he clearly shares that viewpoint.[12] That is, he too holds that God's certifying a messenger establishes that person's right to propose divine doctrine and be recognized by his hearers. The certification which God gives his commissioned messenger is the power of doing miracles in his name. When God reveals himself, he does not merely leave us to deduce his presence from the inadequacy of the human writers as sources of such revelation. He certifies them by miraculous attestation as well. It is especially clear that Jesus' miracles attest a divine messenger. Edwards writes in Miscellany 444 of the raising of Lazarus:

> Now can it be imagined that God would hear an imposter or so order or suffer it that so extraordinary a thing should be done immediately in consequence of the word and act of an imposter upon his asking it of him who was so impudent, when he asked it as to call him Father and tell him that he always heard him and tell him that he spoke thus for this end that others might see that he did indeed give a testimony to his mission and authority by doing of it at his request in such a manner?

Miracles are sometimes in view when they are not specifically mentioned. When, for example, Edwards observes that the Bible prevails though the mighty of the world are often against it, he apparently sees the survival of Scripture itself as a miracle—a kind of literary burning bush.[13] The liberal Arminian Thomas Chubb may have thought miracles improbable and the deist John Toland may have thought them impossible, but for Jonathan Edwards miracles had thoroughly established the Bible so well that any subsequent miracles—if there were any—could not compare with it. The testimony of Scripture was greater than one rising from the dead and returning to this world.[14] The Scripture is "surer than a voice from heaven" because it has established the worldwide church which has a glory compared to which Moses' church (Israel) had none.[15] Though miracles ceased with the apostolic age, the good obtained by the Bible lasts forever, and God never fails his Word.[16] Though the internal evidence for the Scriptures' divinity is overwhelming, God gave corroborating miracles also to prove that men wrote the Bible under supernatural inspiration.[17]

REVELATION AND MYSTERY

Revelation may appear absurd at first, but it is rational enough when examined.[18] In fact, it is revelation that teaches men to grow up and be rational. At this point Edwards tells the story of the thirteen-year-old boy to whom he stated a simple geometrical fact, well known to adults but utterly incredible to the child.[19]

Of course, the biblical revelation *is* mysterious. When the deist John Toland wrote his *Christianity Not Mysterious,* he must, in Edwards' (as in John Locke's) opinion, have been as childish as he was unorthodox. Edwards constantly defends believing the mysterious. "It is not necessary that persons should have clear ideas of the things that are the subject of a proposition in order to their being rationally convinced of the truth of the proposition."[20] He argues that even the heathen knew better than to be confined to the Cartesian principle (the principle that certainty can only come by clear and distinct ideas).

There is no justification in Edwards' theology for Conrad Cherry's statement: "The Scriptures . . . become the Word of God only through the power of God's Spirit."[21] The Devil obviously knows the Bible is the Word of God. Edwards nowhere says or infers that the Bible is not the Word of God unless the reader is illumined by the Holy Spirit, though through the Spirit's illumination the reader does indeed know, in the fullest sense, or is "persuaded" that the Bible is the Word of God. Edwards specifically argues in the Hebrews 5:12 sermon that people are to study the Word of God whether they are illumined or not. As we shall see in the next section, Edwards believed that unregenerate readers do not see the "excellency" of the Word of God—but this is not to say that they do not see that the Bible is the Word of God, for even the devils see this.

THE LIMITATIONS OF REASON

There are at least four basic limitations of human reason. First, it cannot make the knowledge of God "real" to unregenerate man. Second, it cannot yield a supernatural, salvific revelation or even "sense" it by mere reason. Third, if it does receive a revelation, it cannot thereafter determine what that revelation may and may not contain. Fourth, it cannot even "apprehend" divine revelation as divine revelation, though it may recognize its presence.

Arminians think more highly of man than they ought, and their apologists wrongly suppose that man's reasoning is sound enough to bring him to God. This is not Edwards' opinion, however. The Calvinistic Edwards finds fallen men quite capable of seeing the truth they do not love and therefore rejecting it even as they formulate it. As one nineteenth-century Calvinist, W. G. T. Shedd, put it: "The approbation of goodness is not the love of it."[22]

Reason does not necessarily lead us to righteousness. Nor does it necessarily lead us out of every theological problem. There are apparent theological discrepancies in Scripture which Edwards cannot reconcile and which he does not suppose that God expects men to be capable of reconciling. In natural theology, no less than revealed theology, the conception of infinity, for example, is utterly baffling to Edwards. So "to reject everything but what we can first see to be agreeable to our reason tends by degree to bring everything relating not only to revealed religion but even natural religion into doubt."[23] So although revelation must be demonstrable, the attempt to make it always comprehensible would "tend at last, to make men esteem the science of religion as of no value, and so totally neglect it; and from step to step it will lead to skepticism, atheism, ignorance, and at length to barbarity."[24] Thus, according to Edwards, too great a demand for understanding leads at last to no understanding. Yet reason is a useful and necessary tool for any serious Christian, though the believer recognizes that the human mind must be satisfied with its limitations.

THREE
THE TRINITY

Shortly after Edwards' death a rumor began that he had departed from traditional Trinitarian doctrine. In time the matter was cleared, and those who had hoped for one reason or another to find heresy in the great champion of orthodoxy were disappointed.[1]

THE SUSPICION
CONCERNING EDWARDS' ORTHODOXY

We can only speculate on the reason for this ungrounded suspicion concerning Edwards, the same ungrounded rumor that had plagued Calvin in Geneva. Edwards was orthodox on this doctrine from the beginning, as was Calvin. Perhaps the trouble was Edwards' profound way of expressing the traditional doctrine. He raised some doubts because of his idealism, a philosophy which he thought could be expressed in the forms of traditional Christian orthodoxy. One familiar with the history of the doctrine of the Trinity will see nothing aberrant in the Edwardsean formulation. Those less familiar and less inclined to speculation may find it strange, if not Unitarian-sounding, to be sure. It was not the way Puritans usually expressed this foundational teaching, but it was not heretical.

In Miscellany 94 Edwards writes:

> That image of God which God infinitely loves and has his chief delight in, is the perfect idea of God. It has always been said that God's infinite delight consists in reflecting on himself and viewing his own perfections or, which is the same thing, in his own perfect idea of himself, so that 'tis acknowledged that God's infinite love is to and his infinite delight [is] in the perfect image of himself. But the Scriptures tell us that the Son of God is that image.

Edwards seems to see the Son of God existing as *idea* in the mind of God. Edwards will go on to prove that this is one and the same thing, but extracts such as the one above might, when considered apart from Edwards' total work, give the impression that he is not affirming what other Puritan writers stated clearly.

Augustine had expressed the doctrine similarly in his *On the Trinity*, and the Middle Ages had gone along with his work as the orthodox formulation. Whether Edwards compared himself with the Augustinian tradition or not, he was aware of it in Chevalier Ramsey's work, from which he quoted at great length (in Miscellany 1253) with apparent approval. R. A. Delattre notes how Edwards had from the beginning conceived this love between the Father and his Idea, the son, as substantial.[2] Edwards addresses this matter of substance in Miscellany 94:

> The perfect act of God must be a substantial act. . . . The perfect delights of reasonable creatures are substantial delights, but the delight of God is [much more] properly a substance, yea, an infinitely perfect substance, even the essence.

THE OCCASION FOR
EDWARDS' TRINITARIAN FORMULATION

Deists and Unitarians believed the doctrine of the Trinity could be easily dispensed with. Their thought left no room for the divinity of Christ and the Spirit. The orthodox doctrine of the Trinity was being challenged, and Edwards must have felt called upon to rise to its defense. The prevailing reason in the church for still holding to the doctrine was that the atonement required the deity of Christ and sanctification required the power of the Third Person of the Godhead, the Spirit. In other words, the doctrine was believed mostly for pragmatic reasons — sinful man needed a divine Savior (the Son) and a divine Sanctifier (the Spirit), and the Trinity was a tidy explanation of the three-personed God. Edwards the thinker knew that the doctrine should be believed because it explained so much about the nature of God. With the doctrine of the Trinity sinking to the utility of the economic Trinity exclusively, a great need to reassert and defend the underlying essential Trinity became evident. If this could not be done, Edwards sensed that the economic Trinity, with which he was greatly concerned himself, could not long continue.[3]

Edwards surely felt early the urgency of defending this basic Christian doctrine, although he never published a treatise on the subject. Such a treatise was printed posthumously. But in his very early Miscellany 94 Edwards gives what may have been not only his fullest single development of the doctrine, but also a basic statement of it from which he never departed. The rest of his entries in the Miscellanies, sermons, and especially the *Treatise on Grace* amount to a filling out of important details and proofs of the doctrine originally presented.

THE METAPHYSICAL
FOUNDATION OF THE DOCTRINE

Even before Miscellany 94, however, Edwards had laid the foundation for the doctrine in "Excellence," his first entry in *The Mind:* "But in a being that is absolutely without any plurality, there cannot be excellence, for there can be no such thing as consent or agreement."[4] Since harmony with being is essential to excellence and excellence is essential to the concept of God, God must have harmony, and harmony requires plurality of persons. So, for God to be excellent he must be multi-personal. Later Edwards went into more detail on this fascinating theme. God's love of himself is equal to his love of, or consent to, all being. So love of himself is the begetting of the Son, and this "mutual love" makes the third, the personal Holy Spirit (Miscellany 94).

Miscellany 94 was written about 1722, possibly before *The Mind* and well before the beginning of the ministry in Northampton in 1727. Edwards begins in a polemic tone, observing that "there has been much cry of late against saying one word particularly about the Trinity but what the Scripture has said, judging it impossible but that, if we did, we should err in a question so much above us." Edwards disagrees vigorously, believing that it is within the "reach of naked reason to perceive certainly that there are three, distinct [persons] in God, each of which is the same [God]" (Miscellany 94).

THE BEGETTING OF THE SON

We have seen something of Edwards' handling of the Trinitarian doctrine in general terms. He does not neglect the individual persons in the Godhead either. While saying less about the Father and much more about the Son, he pays greatest attention and makes his greatest contribution to the concept of the Spirit.

However, he has much to say about the Son. In Miscellany 117 Edwards writes that from all eternity there must have been an object which God infinitely loves. "Otherwise He could not be happy, because happiness is consent to Being or God. Therefore, this other Being must be of the same essence as Himself."

Edwards sees many analogies of the Trinity in nature: the sun, the rainbow, and especially man. There is yet more of an image of the Trinity in the soul of man. There is the mind, its understanding (or idea), and the will (or affection) corresponding to God, the Idea of God (the Son), and the love of God (the Spirit) (Miscellany 390).

Edwards begins his speculation on the Trinity with the accepted notion that God is infinitely happy from eternity. Since the divine way of knowing is not essentially different from ours, God's delight too must be in the ideas he has. But what idea could satisfy an infinite being except the idea of an infinite being, which is himself? This idea is his image. His son is born eternally by the Father's beholding himself. So convinced is Edwards of his reasoning that he concludes that, if the word *begotten* had not been used elsewhere in Scripture, it would have been used in this case because "there is no other word that so properly expresses it" (Miscellany 94).

THE PROCESSION OF THE SPIRIT

Out of this relation between the Father and the Son, the Holy Spirit eternally proceeds:

> The Holy Spirit is the act of God between the Father and the Son, infinitely loving and delighting in each other. If the Father and the

> Son do infinitely delight in each other, there must be an infinitely
> pure and perfect act between them, an infinitely sweet energy
> which we call delight. This is certainly distinct from the other
> two. . . . It is distinct from each of the other two, and yet it is God. It
> is in the Spirit that God is eternal and pure act. (Miscellany 94)

Edwards' *Treatise on Grace* relates the doctrine of the Holy
Spirit, on the one hand, to the inner mystery of the divine nature, and on the other to the spiritual life of man. The Holy
Spirit comes into his own in this treatise, although especially
in relation to sanctification.

Edwards has an interesting explanation in Miscellany 223
of the apparent omission of the Holy Spirit from the Trinity
in the benediction of 2 Corinthians 13:14.

> The Apostle's blessing, wherein he wishes "the grace of the Lord Je-
> sus Christ, the love of the Father, and the communion of the Holy
> Ghost" (2 Cor. 13:14), contains not different things but is simple: 'tis
> the same blessing, even the Spirit of God, which is the comprehen-
> sion of all happiness. Therefore, the Apostle in his blessing to the
> Corinthians (1 Cor. 16:23-24) says, "The grace of our Lord Jesus
> Christ be with you. My love be with you in Christ Jesus. Amen." —
> Christian love being the communication of Christ's love, and the
> Holy Ghost dwelling in us.

It should be fairly obvious that Edwards was quite orthodox in his thought regarding the Trinity. What should also be
obvious is that, like the other great theologians of the
church, he sought creative, insightful ways of expressing
Trinitarian doctrine. Certainly the Trinity is not easy to understand; indeed, perhaps it is never really within man's
grasp. Edwards would surely agree that the depths of the divine mystery — including the very essence of God — cannot
be plumbed by mortal man. But, armed with his reason, his
devotion to scriptural truth, and his own ability to express
thought creatively, Edwards sought to explain to his contem-
poraries — and to later generations — the three-personed
God and the relationships within the Godhead.

FOUR
MAN AND HIS FALL

The great problem with the Edwardsean view of man is how man made in the image of God could ever become man the sinner. On this problem we will concentrate in this brief chapter.

Edwards, along with all Christians and the Bible itself, teaches that man the good creature of God did indeed become man the sinner. The usual explanation is that man became a sinner by his free will. But this explains nothing, because the real question is *why* man chose to become man the sinner. How could a good creature of God do an evil thing?

If anyone ever tried to untie this theological knot, it was Jonathan Edwards. The young Edwards wrote:

> If it be enquired how man came to sin, seeing he had no sinful inclinations in him, except God took away his grace from him that he had been wont to give him and so let him fall, I answer there was no need of taking away any that had been given him, but he sin'd under that temptation because God did not give him more. He did not take away that grace from him while he was perfectly innocent which grace was his original righteousness, but he only withheld his confirming grace given now in heaven, grace as shall surmount every temptation. . . . (Miscellany 290)

There are problems with this explanation, of course. Edwards tries to escape his own snare by restating the situation with different language. He insists that man succumbed because God "did not give him more" grace. God was willing to give him more *if* man had asked for it.

But that, of course, was the temptation—not to ask and trust God. Edwards is saying that man did not meet the temptation not to ask for more because God "did not give him more." That is, man needed more grace to ask for more. God "withheld his confirming grace." ("Confirming grace" refers to grace which would certainly establish man in his original righteousness.) The "sufficient" grace Adam had was insufficient to get what was unfailingly sufficient: confirming grace.[1]

Edwards tries to explain this in Miscellany 436:

> And this must be what is meant when we say that God gave our first parent sufficient grace tho he withheld an efficacious grace or a grace that should certainly uphold him in all temptations he could meet with. I say this must be meant by his having sufficient grace viz that he had grace sufficient to render him a free agent not only with respect to his whole will but with respect to his rational or the will that arose from a rational judgment of what was indeed best for himself.

Sufficient grace was, he continues, "sufficient to render him a free agent . . . with respect to . . . the will that arose from a rational judgment . . . of what was indeed best for himself." Edwards must mean by "free agent" an *able* agent and not merely a potentially able agent. But that is exactly what he denied. Sufficient grace was not enough to render man an able agent. Only confirming grace could do that.

Does this mean man was put in such a position that, once tempted by the serpent, he had no choice but to sin? If this were so, it means man is, ultimately, not responsible for his fall. Once again Edwards tries to recoup the situation by showing how Adam did in fact sin when it might have been otherwise. "Man might be deceived so that he should not be disposed to use his endeavors to persevere but if he did use his endeavours there was sufficient assistance always with him to enable him to persevere" (Miscellany 501). But how could man have been deceived if he had a natural understanding sufficient to comprehend the difference between a command of the Creator and a temptation of a creature? If he did not, how could he be held responsible?

Here Edwards tries to explain why Adam did not endeavor to persevere (ask for confirming grace). We have stated above that man would have to have confirming grace to endeavor with it. Here Edwards says that Adam was deceived so as not to be disposed to persevere. If man could be deceived by another creature (the serpent), he did not have sufficient grace to cope. He needed confirming grace, but he was capable of being deceived so as to think he did not.

Nathaniel Emmons says that Edwards on one occasion was like a great horse stuck in the mud. The more he struggled to extricate himself, the deeper he sank. I am afraid this is the case here.

Therefore, when Edwards says that Adam had sufficient grace to choose in accord with mere rational judgment, does that mean anything other than this: If Adam would call upon this grace he would be able to choose in accord with his rational judgment regardless of his appetites? But, if fallen man would *now* call upon grace, would he not also be able to choose in accord with his mere rational judgment? There is no possibility that fallen man will, of himself, call upon the grace of God. But was there any possibility that unfallen man would do so if inclined otherwise (as in fact he was), being overwhelmed by his appetite and corrupted judgment? If unfallen man or fallen man would call on the efficacious or sufficient grace of God, he would be able to stand against all temptation; if not, neither fallen nor unfallen man would be able to do so; and neither was able to call on the grace of God unless inclined to do so which neither was so inclined at the time of sin. What is the difference?

According to Edwards, the difference between unfallen and fallen man in this regard is that unfallen man had sufficient grace naturally available to choose according to his mere rational judgment, while fallen man does not. It comes down to this: Unfallen man could have been inclined to choose according to his rational judgment; fallen man cannot. But this, being interpreted, simply means that if unfallen man found that his mere rational judgment seemed good to him he could choose it; if not, he could not. But the same is true of fallen man. Suppose Edwards says: But the mere rational judgment might have seemed good to the unfallen man but never to the fallen man. But, we have seen that that is not the case, and could not have been without confirming grace. So, again, what real difference is there between the fallen and unfallen will? Where is the greater freedom of will in unfallen man?

Other Reformed theologians had said the same as Edwards. They, too, explained the greater freedom of Adam by his sufficient ability to choose the good and his descendants' lack of it. Augustine is famous for his terms *posse peccare* (able to sin) and *posse non peccare* (able not to sin). These other Reformed theologians seem content to let the matter rest there. Thus, they never exposed themselves. They were satisfied merely to assert. Edwards always attempts to explain. That is when the nakedness of this imperial doctrine is exposed. To change the metaphor: if the whale did not spout off it would not be harpooned.

In one of the last Miscellanies he ever wrote, Edwards was

still struggling. In Miscellany 1394 he has slipped so deeply as to suggest that the rational judgment of created man could be overpowered by the sensibility so that man yielding to that sinned, as Adam did, with his eyes open. In the very next Miscellany (1395) he contends that man's rational judgment must be perverted before he can sin!

Nevertheless, the great horse sinks to the bottom in his very greatest intellectual effort, the *Freedom of the Will* itself. Here we read his thoughts concerning sin's first entrance into the world:

> It was meet, if sin did come into existence and appear in the world, it should arise from the imperfection which properly belongs to a creature, as such, and should appear so to do, that it might appear not to be from God as the efficient or fountain. *But this could not have been, if man had been made at first with sin in his heart;* nor unless the abiding principle and habit of sin were first introduced by an evil act of the creature. If sin had not arisen from the imperfection of the creature, it would not have been so visible, that it did not arise from God, as the positive cause, and real source of it.[2]

Edwards makes another futile effort to extricate himself from the pit into which he sank. In *Original Sin* he explains that Adam did not have to have a fixed inclination to sin in order to commit one sin of disobedience. What difference does it make whether he had to have a "fixed" or "permanent" inclination? He had to have *an* inclination to evil and that could only have come from the Creator.

As did Noah, Edwards became "drunk" on one occasion in spite of a life of exceptional holiness. And just as in the case of Noah, there was undoubtedly powerful temptation; so here the great intellectual theologian became intoxicated with the greatest theological problem in the entire Word of God.

If we ordinary Christians have not been overcome, it is be-

cause we have not felt as keenly the almost irresistible temptation to solve the unsolvable. We have been spared not because we are better, but because it has been easier for us to
realize that this problem is beyond us.

FIVE
SIN

When man sinned he lost all the beauty of his nature. There is nothing left but a filthy and devilish nature that reigns in the hearts of natural men. Edwards constantly preached that man is devoid of the love and presence of God and that this is the root of all evil. We learn from *Original Sin* that God withdrew when Adam rebelled, and this occasioned man's natural corruption. No infusion or transfusion of corruption was necessary.

The theme was developed in the manuscript sermon on Genesis 3:11.[1] Nothing more was needed to explain the invariable and incorrigible wickedness of mankind than privation of the love of God. Man's evil actions begin at birth and continue through life.[2] Environment and example make no difference because the cause is internal.

The Matthew 10:17 sermon is an especially vivid description of the brutality and cruelty that can be accounted for by the mere absence of God in the soul. "The nature of man is so corrupted that he is become a very evil and hurtful creature."[3] Many other sermons are like it. For example, the Romans 5:10 sermon makes it clear that man, being devoid of the divine presence, does indeed actively hate God.[4] Men do not admit it (one thinks of the remark of Henry David Thoreau: "I am not at war with God"), but they are the sworn enemies of God.

In fact, man the sinner claims to be at peace and friendly, but he is at peace with false gods. All true religion professed by unregenerates is "forced."[5] Men do not attack God openly because he is out of their reach, just as a serpent will not strike at a person who is at a distance.[6] But men's actions show clearly how they feel. God is placed below the world in their scale of values; even vile lusts are placed above God.[7] There is actually a never-ending struggle going on between God and man to see who will be chief.[8] Human worms raise themselves up in defiance of their Creator, and this is why all unconverted persons are wicked and unable to escape the damnation of hell.[9] Jeremiah 44:4 teaches that sinners hate God,[10] Habakkuk 1:13 that God hates sinners,[11] and Zechariah 11:8 that there is mutual loathing.[12] Man's heart without God is as a stone, and God hardens it only by withdrawing further and further.[13] Needless to say, it is futile for the sinner to argue that God is to blame for hardening his heart, for man's heart becomes hardened only when God is absent.[14]

Christianity and Christian culture make the world still more sinful if the faith is not savingly embraced, as usually it is not. Consequently, the Indians ("savage Americans" in Edwards' terminology), though suffering from original sin, are less wicked than those who conquered them, as is characteristic of the whole history of this fallen world. The "cutflower" civilization Elton Trueblood spoke of turns out to be a garden of weeds:

> And as to the Gentile nations, though there was a glorious success of the gospel amongst them in the Apostles' days; yet probably not one in ten of those that had the gospel preached to them embraced

it. . . . And the greater part of the ages which have now elapsed have been spent in the duration of that grand and general apostasy, under which the Christian world, as it is called, has been transformed into that which has been vastly more deformed, more dishonorable and hateful to God, and repugnant to true virtue, than the state of the heathen world before: which is agreeable to the prophetical descriptions given of it by the Holy Spirit.[15]

ORIGINAL SIN IS UNIVERSAL, INCLUDING INFANTS

The most tragic evidence of this universal disobedience is not the heathen nations, the savage Americans, and the secularized Christian culture, but the human infant. Edwards exhaustively gathers the texts to show that the Word of God finds infants under condemnation:

Here, not to stay to be particular concerning the command by Moses, concerning the destruction of the infants of the Midianites (Num. 31:17). And that given to Saul to destroy all the infants of the Amalekites (1 Sam. 15:3), and what is said concerning Edom (Ps. 137:9), "Happy shall he be that shall take thy little ones, and dash them against the stones." I proceed to take notice of something remarkable concerning the destruction of Jerusalem, represented in Ezekiel 9, when command was given to them that had charge over the city, to destroy the inhabitants (vv. 1-8). And this reason is given for it, that their iniquity required it, and it was a just recompence of their sin (vv. 9, 10). . . . Command was given to the angel, to go through the city, and set a mark upon their foreheads, and the destroying angel had a strict charge not to come near any man on whom was the mark; yet the infants were not marked, nor a word said of sparing them: on the contrary, infants were expressly mentioned as those that should be utterly destroyed, without pity (vv. 5, 6). "Go . . . through the city, and smite: let not your eye spare, neither have ye pity. Slay utterly old and young, both maids, and little children, and women: but come not near any man upon whom is the mark."[16]

Edwards continues: "No care was taken to preserve the infants of the city." He concludes that they were involved in that destruction just as the children to whom Christ alludes when he says of the coming tribulation: "Blessed are the barren, and the womb that never bare, and the paps which never gave suck."

All the above is direct evidence that the Bible teaches the condemnation of children in Adam. Edwards cites some negative evidence also which is, perhaps, even more impressive. He observes that God has offered Abraham to spare Sodom if there were but ten righteous in the city. There were not, though there must have been more than that many infants. Nor is Edwards insensitive to the contrary appeal to Christ's taking the children in his arms and saying that of such is the kingdom of heaven. For Edwards, these children are no more virtuous than the doves who have that same image. Grimly he reminds his readers that vipers too, when young, are cute and harmless, though their malignant nature will later appear clearly. If this doctrine is considered harsh, Wesley's Arminianism did not save him from it either, for he, too, argued that since children suffer they must deserve to suffer.

DISOBEDIENCE UNIVERSALLY

Not only is mankind disobedient universally, but its disobedience is universal. That is, not only is disobedience as extensive as mankind, but it pertains to each individual in the universality of his being. The totality of mankind is totally depraved according to Edwards, who, if anything, is more thoroughgoing than John Calvin on this crucial Calvinistic doctrine. For Edwards, though the image of God in the broader sense is intact, the image in the narrower or proper sense is utterly eradicated.

Lacking all virtue, there is nothing men do (according to numerous sermons) that is good.[17] In fact, all that they do is wrong.[18] Their minds are carnal,[19] and their bodies are the sepulchres of their dead minds.[20] Their life's trade, or business, is sin.[21] There is always room for further wickedness and only the common grace of God limits it. Men are so wicked that when Christ first told his disciples to beware of wolves he changed it to say beware of men because men are far more ferocious and cruel than animals.[22]

SIN INVOLVES INFINITE GUILT

Edwards maintains that virtue does not have finite merit,[23] but sin has infinite demerit:

> There is no great merit in paying a debt we owe, and by the highest possible obligations in strict justice are obliged to pay; but there is great demerit in refusing to pay it. That on such accounts as these there is an infinite demerit in all sin against God which must therefore immensely outweigh all the merit which can be supposed to be in our virtue, I think, is capable of full demonstration; and that the futility of the objections, which some have made against the argument, might most plainly be demonstrated.[24]

Sin is against an infinitely worthy being and is therefore infinitely heinous. Every sin, according to Edwards, is an infinite aggravation against an infinitely holy God.[25] He observes in many sermons that an offense against an excellent person is doubtless more serious than against a less excellent person. By a straight line of logical reasoning he concludes that a sin against an infinitely excellent person is an infinitely heinous deed. Even more clearly he states in the Matthew 25:46 sermon that "if the obligation to love, honor and obey God be infinite, then sin, which is the violation of this obligation, is a violation of infinite obligation, and so is an infinite evil." The same theme is fundamental in *Justification by Faith*:

We are under greater obligations to love a more lovely being than a less lovely; and if a being be infinitely excellent and lovely, our obligations to love him are therein infinitely great. . . . The unworthiness of sin or opposition to God rises and is great in proportion to the dignity of the object and inferiority of the subject; but on the contrary, the value of respect rises in proportion to the value of the subject. . . . [26]

Likewise, in one of his most famous sermons, Edwards labors this point in establishing the "justice of God in the damnation of sinners":

Every crime or fault deserves a greater or less punishment, in proportion as the crime itself is greater or less. . . . The faulty nature of anything is the formal ground and reason of its desert of punishment; and therefore the more anything hath of this nature, the more punishment it deserves. And therefore the terribleness of the degree of punishment, let it be never so terrible, is no argument against the justice of it, if the proportion does but hold. . . .

A crime is more or less heinous, according as we are under greater or less obligations to the contrary. . . . So the faultiness of one being hating another, is in proportion to his obligation to love him. . . . And therefore if there be any being that we are under infinite obligations to love, and honour, and obey, the contrary towards him must be infinitely faulty. Our obligation to love, honour, and obey any being, is in proportion to his loveliness, honourableness, and authority; for that is the very meaning of the words. When we say anyone is very lovely, it is the same as to say, that he is one very much to be loved. . . .

So that sin against God, being a violation of infinite obligations, must be a crime infinitely heinous, and so deserving infinite punishment.[27]

"MORAL" MEN ARE UTTERLY SINFUL

Joseph G. Haroutunian has written what is one of the most interesting studies of Edwardsean and New England theology.[28] It is titled *Piety Versus Moralism*, and that very title states its theme: New England theology after Edwards turned away from theology—and piety—to a mere moralism. What he says is undoubtedly true, but there is a deficiency in Haroutunian's understanding of "moralism" in Edwards. He seems to think that though Edwards does not deny that the natural man may be good, Edwards will not permit himself to lose sight of the fact that to be religious and to be moral are indeed two different things. What Haroutunian does not seem to realize is that, for Jonathan Edwards, to be truly moral without being religious is impossible.

Outward morality is, of course, possible and sometimes highly cultivated by some human sinners; but real morality is something else again. In his sermon on Romans 3:11, Edwards preached: "When they (natural men) do an act of justice it is not wrong as an act of justice and when they do an act of liberality is it not wrong as an act of liberality. . . . What is done is only a shadow without substance. There is the shell of the duty but the inside is hollow."[29] The natural man may have a "shadow" of morality, but never the real thing.

Edwards puts the same principle in somewhat more technical language:

> Thus when a natural man speaks the truth, when he is just in his dealings, when he gives to the poor, he does those things that are right as to the matter of them though altogether wrong as to the manner. As to what is visible in the action it is right. That which is as it were the body of the actions; but, if we look at the inward principle and aim which is, as it were, the soul of the act and is what God looks at and which the rule does chiefly regard it is altogether wrong.[30]

Again, he says in the same unpublished sermons (surely some of the most important ethical deliverances he ever wrote) that natural men do what is "negatively and comparatively right, i.e., that they may do those things whereby they avoid those things that are much more wrong."[31] There are, after all, degrees of sinfulness even where there is no true virtue present. "They can avoid many sins."[32] Again, "when natural men do avoid wilfully doing that which is directly contrary to a known command of God they may be said to do right. . . . 'Tis not in itself so wrong as what they avoid. . . . The path that a man walks in may be comparatively straight as compared with some other paths but yet the path he goes in may be notwithstanding indeed crooked. Of crooked paths there may be a great deal of difference. Some may be much less crooked than others and so as to avoid many great crooks that are in others (yet) 'tis not straight."[33] There are, we would say, bad good works; bad as to motive, good as to appearance.

In a sermon which carries the title "Wicked Men Are the Children of Hell," Edwards remarks that "there are many in a natural condition that are a very good sort of man, are sober and moral in their behavior. . . ."[34] Of course, he means moral in the sense of outwardly moral, because Edwards would never say that truly moral men are children of hell.

Likewise, in a sermon entitled "The Gadarenes Loved Their Swine Better Than Jesus Christ," Edwards says that if natural men ever part with anything it is not for Christ's sake but to avoid hell. So the morality of swinish people is really centered on hell, not toward heaven.[35]

The famous metaphors of Edwards about the soul-destroying character of even one sin have led Haroutunian to suppose that Edwards believed natural men were capable of true morality. We will skip the one in which Edwards mentions that if a boat crossing the Atlantic only sank once it would nevertheless be fatal and cite this one about a servant and a wife:

> Therefore how absurd must it be for Christians to object against the depravity of man's nature, a greater number of innocent and kind

actions, than of crimes; and to talk of a prevailing innocency, good nature, industry and cheerfulness of the greater part of mankind? Infinitely more absurd, than it would be to insist that the domestic of a prince was not a bad servant because though sometimes he condemned and affronted his master to a great degree yet he did not spit in his master's face so often as he performed acts of service; or than it would be to affirm, that his spouse was a good wife to him, because, although she committed adultery, and that with the slaves and scoundrels sometimes, yet she did not do this so often as she did the duties of a wife.[36]

Since most people cannot see little sins and must be, as it were, hit over the head with gross ones, Edwards is vividly pointing out that one sin would be enough to vitiate the morality of any person. If a servant only spit in his master's face once a year, this would surely label him a bad servant no matter how impeccable his behavior the rest of the time. Edwards never for a moment supposes that there is any time when any man does anything truly virtuous, even though most of the time most men abstain from the gross, conspicuous acts of immorality. Because man is basically sinful in all he does, the atonement is necessary.

SIX

ATONEMENT

"The necessity of Christ's satisfaction to divine justice is, as it were, the center and hinge of all doctrines of pure revelation. Other doctrines are of little importance comparatively except as they have respect to this."[1] This quotation gives some indication of the importance Edwards attributed to the doctrine of atonement. Although scattered throughout his writings rather than concentrated in one definitive treatise, Edwards' thinking on the atonement is comprehensive as well as profound. His doctrine was followed almost immediately by a deviation from Reformed orthodoxy among his followers, beginning with his son. Nevertheless, he himself was an orthodox Anselmian, going beyond the great medieval theologian in his characteristic penetration. We will briefly note here his treatment of the necessity, nature, and design of the atonement, and the Trinitarian involvement in it, concluding with a hint about Edwards' relation to the governmental, or Grotian, theory.

THE NECESSITY OF THE ATONEMENT

Edwards argues the necessity of sacrifice from the fact that sacrificing has existed throughout the world. It is a common conviction that man should not be pardoned without sacrifice. Though heathen sacrifices have no value, they do point to a true sacrifice.

The sermon "The Necessity and Reasonableness of the Atonement" represents the holiness of God as disposing him to punish sin. His justice made atonement necessary if he were to pardon sin. The emphasis in that basic work is on the necessity of God's keeping his word rather than vindicating his justice.

The heart of Edwards' doctrine of the atonement is his doctrine of the necessity of satisfaction, and it is defended in the lengthy Miscellany 779. We will begin with a brief summary of this, "The Necessity and Reasonableness of Satisfaction."

Justice requires that sin be punished because it deserves punishment.

> None will deny that some crimes are so horrid and deserving of punishment, that it is requisite that they should not go unpunished unless something very considerable be done to make up for the crime; either some answerable repentance or some other compensation that in some measure at least balances the desert of punishment . . . otherwise . . . it is fit and becoming, and to be desired, that the crime should be severely punished on no other account but because they deserve it.

It will follow that God should punish all sin with infinite punishment unless there be "other compensation." But there can be no infinite repentance by the creature. In any case, there is no proportion between human repentance and guilt. If anyone asks why God could not pardon on the basis of repentance, Edwards claims that the answer is the same as why God could not do so without man's repentance. "For all the repentance men are capable of, is no repentance at all"

(Miscellany 779).[2] Actually we are forgiven for repentance only because it has respect to "compensation already made," the death of Christ.

Furthermore, it is fit that a person's state of punishment should be proportionate to his disposition. "This is what the consciences of all men do naturally declare" (Miscellany 779).[3]

The holiness of God, which is the infinite opposition of his nature to sin, "naturally and necessarily disposes him to punish sin" (Miscellany 779).[4] Holiness is hatred of sin; justice (a part of holiness) is hatred of the disconnection of sin and punishment. Indignation is the proper expression of the enmity against sin or, which is the same thing, against the faultiness or blameworthiness of moral agents. Therefore, taking vengeance is a proper divine expression of this hatred of sin.

"Justice to himself requires that God should punish sin with infinite punishment" (Miscellany 779).[5] The "language of sin" is man's disdain, which requires a divine demonstration against it by the Supreme Governor.

The necessity of punishment follows from the law of God which threatens it. There may be stipulated exceptions to law, but no dispensations for several reasons. First, dispensations would destroy law, which must be "fixed." Second, law was made to destroy sin, not to be destroyed by sin. Third, annulment of God's law implies "want of wisdom and foresight or some defect." Fourth, the sacredness of the authority and majesty of the lawgiver makes enforcement of the law necessary; "though, strictly speaking, he is not obliged to execute because he has threatened, yet he was obliged not absolutely to threaten, if he at the same time knew that he should not and could not execute."[6]

Hence, if any sinner is ever to be reconciled to God an adequate atonement is absolutely necessary.

THE NATURE OF THE ATONEMENT:
CHRIST'S ACTIVE AND PASSIVE OBEDIENCE

Seventeenth-century Reformed orthodoxy had a well-developed doctrine of the active and passive obedience of Christ. It was clear that man the sinner was required by God's law to be punished for infractions and to fulfill the law's demands in order to be acceptable to the Lawgiver.[7] Since both of these had to be performed by man, who was incapable of either, reconciliation could come about only by the God-man. He redeemed man by suffering the punishment and by fulfilling the demands of the law. The former was his passive obedience, the latter his active obedience.

The orthodox were at pains to teach that Christ's passive obedience (suffering) was not sufficient. At first it seems to have been thought that the active obedience (resisting temptation and fulfilling the demands of the law) was for Christ's own sake (to earn him life and qualify him for his passive obedience). Later it was clearly maintained that if Christ did fulfill the law for himself as a natural human obligation, this was also on behalf of the elect as well.[8]

In Edwards the inseparability of Christ's active and passive obedience is constantly stressed and developed. "Every act of obedience was propitiatory and every act of obedience was meritorious. Christ's principal suffering was also an *act* of obedience" (Miscellany 845). (Hebrews 5:8 is cited.) The blood of Christ is probably spoken of no less often as sweet and acceptable as propitiatory (Isa. 53; John 10:17, 18; Acts 20:28; Rom. 5:9; Eph. 2:13; 5:2). The blood of Christ washes away guilt, while it is the Spirit of Christ who washes away pollution. However, it is the blood of Christ which purchases the Spirit and sanctification. Thus, in the Old Testament, sacrifices were called sweet savors on both accounts: obedience bound with sacrifice. Christ's sacrifice was a great testimony to God's majesty and at the same time a marvelous act of obedience.

Edwards has no doubt that all of Christ's active obedience was on man's account. Christ's becoming man did not in itself make him a proper redeemer because he remained God. But since he voluntarily made himself a servant, his obedience was purely meritorious for mankind. Everything Christ performed in man's stead is accepted for man. All he did as mediator was done on behalf of man, and all his obedience accrues to man.

Edwards then proves that the sacrifice must be an infinite one, since sacrifice must be proportionate to the offense. If no equivalence was necessary, man could be forgiven without any sacrifice.

Christ's active/passive obedience was chiefly manifested in his last sufferings as they openly honored God. These sufferings of his sacrificial death were absolutely necessary because grace could only come through them. "For though indeed the covenant of grace was of force before the death of Christ, yet it was of force no other wise than by his death. . . . "[9]

Perhaps Edwards' most exquisite discussion of his Savior's sufferings is found in Miscellany 1005. Christ, unlike sinners, Edwards says, bore the wrath of God knowing that God loved him. Still, he experienced the dreadfulness of the infinite wrath of God against sinners and how much they deserved punishment. "Christ's great love and pity to the elect (that his offering up himself on the cross was the greatest act and fruit of, and consequently which he was then in the highest exercise of) was one source of his suffering . . . " (Miscellany 1005). Christ's love brought his elect infinitely near to him in that great act and suffering wherein he stood for them.

From this a couple of corollaries are drawn. First, the very bitterness of the cup caused Christ to go on and drink it all, because, seeing the dreadfulness of sin, he was determined to take it himself. His "pity towards his elect" moved him to deliver them by his suffering. Second, his aversion to the dreadfulness of sin also caused him to sanctify himself (Miscellany 1005).

Another effect is that God forsook Christ (withholding his love, which was as terrible as the knowledge of his hatred is to the damned) and delivered him to Satan.[10] In all this "God dealt with him as if he had been exceedingly angry with him, as though he had been the object of his dreadful wrath" (Miscellany 1005).

The essence of Edwards' atonement teaching is this: that the justice of God requires the punishment of sin and that the sufferings of the divine Son alone could make mercy compatible with this inexorable divine justice.

To the same effect are a number of similar statements spanning the entirety of Edwards' life such as Miscellanies 6, 245, 281, 350, 398, 846, 898, 912, 918, 1035, 1214, and many sermons, such as those on Revelation 1:5 and 14:13.

According to the unpublished sermon on Hebrews 9: 13, 14, Christ, being both God and man, was the only priest who could offer the necessary atonement. It was essential that he be man: "It is needful that this which represents him that sinned in suffering for him should be the same nature that sinned and deserved suffering. Otherwise the nature that sinned is not punished and so the threatening of the law is not fulfilled which says, 'In the day thou eatest thou shalt die,' . . . " Edwards continues, saying: "If Christ . . . had taken up some other nature such as the nature of angels to suffer, in that he would not have answered the needs of mankind. . . . 'Wherefore in all things it behooved him to be made like unto his brethren. . . . ' " Christ was also without spot or blemish, as all acceptable sacrifices were required to be.

Most important and unique of all, Christ's human nature was sacrificed on the altar of his divine nature. "In order to a sacrifice being acceptable and valid it was necessary not only that it should be offered up at God's altar. There was but one altar of burnt offerings. . . . The altar of burnt offerings was a type of the divine nature of Christ which is the altar on which Christ offered up the sacrifice of his human nature which was greater than the gift which was being offered" (Matt. 23:19).[11] It was the deity of Christ that gave infinite value and virtue to his sufferings.

THE DESIGN OF THE ATONEMENT

What was the design of the infinitely precious atonement? William Cunningham searched the entire corpus of John Calvin's writings and found only two explicit references to the specific design of the atonement. Jonathan Edwards was much more explicit about the limited design of Christ's atonement.

As early as Miscellany 21, Edwards had stated this doctrine negatively (denying that Christ died for the nonelect) and positively (affirming that Christ died for the elect): "Christ did not intend to save those he knew he would not save. If he intended to save any it was those he knew would be saved." In a 1741 sermon, Edwards preached that Christ "has died for them (the elect) and not for the world."[12]

Also, the atonement doctrine is implicit in the divine decrees. God eternally decreed to save some people, the elect. It was the elect that Christ came to save. Since God eternally decreed not to save others, Christ would not be engaged in a fool's errand.

Christ knew what his reward would be. Certain souls were given him for the saving. Even universal redemptionists must see the folly of supposing that Christ would shed his blood not knowing whether he would receive any souls for his hire.

Edwards often speaks of Christ dying for believers. Christ had a dying love for every particular believer. Every believer has as much benefit as if Christ died for him alone.[13] In this very connection Edwards once again notes the "nonsense" of thinking that Christ died for those he knew would not believe.

Edwards does not hesitate to state the design of Christ's redemption as limited to *believers* because in his theology, they are synonymous with *elect*. Even more frequently, he specifies them as *predestined*. "The Father sent forth Christ into the world on this errand to redeem such a number of the children of men and to bring them home to God. . . ."[14] Edwards sees this errand as "the joy that was set before him to redeem and make happy the souls of his elect and he will rejoice therefore when he sees this accomplished."[15] Christ's "love was such to his elect that he came down to dwell on earth." Indeed, "the coming of Christ to die for the elect is the principal manifestation of [the Father's] love to 'em."[16] "Christ doth not vouchsafe so much as to pray for the non-elect, much less did he undergo the cursed death of the cross for them" (John 17:6). Edwards is explicit: "He has died for them and not for the world."[17]

ECONOMIC TRINITY IN THE ATONEMENT

Augustine in his *On the Trinity* observed the full participation of the entire Trinity in the work of atonement. Edwards was concerned to show the same Trinitarian involvement. From his first published sermon, "God Glorified in Man's Dependence," throughout his Miscellanies, and especially in the *Treatise on Grace*, all of the Godhead is involved in all of the work of the atonement. Our dependence is equally on each person in the Trinity, the Father being the provider, Christ the purchaser, who purchased the Spirit, the sanctifier. Edwards' special stress is on the Spirit, the One purchased for man by the atonement.

It is interesting that Louis Berkhof should write: "The history of New England theology reveals a downward trend in the doctrine of the atonement."[18] It is not surprising that, following a lead sentence such as that, he omits all reference to Edwards, who gives us a major orthodox treatment of the atonement.[19]

Nevertheless, in Miscellany 306 Edwards does sound as if a "downward trend" had occurred. According to 306, if God did not punish sin, "nobody could charge God with any wrong." How could an Anselmian like Edwards say that? While we are perplexed by this, pure governmentalism follows fast. "As God's nature inclines him [to] order all things beautifully properly and decently, so it was necessary that sin should be punished." He continues, "There is this necessity, besides what arises from the veracity of God." In other words, while the punishment of sin is necessary, it has a necessity from governmental propriety and veracity, inasmuch as God has said that he will punish sin.

Edwards was, like most Puritan thinkers, an Anselmian — that is, he held to the satisfaction theory of the atonement. According to Anselm, sin is dishonoring the majesty of God, the sovereign, so satisfaction must be offered. Christ, through his death and suffering, offers satisfaction to the offended God. Hugo Grotius (1583–1645) propounded the so-called governmental theory, which claims that Christ suffered as a penal example, whereby the holy law was honored while sinners were pardoned. The death of Christ was a public example of the depth of sin and how far God would go to uphold the moral order of the universe.

Some later New England theologians championed the

governmental (Grotian) theory of the atonement, thinking they had Jonathan Edwards as father. It is statements such as the above and the following that gave birth to such notions, yet without justification. In Edwards' sermon on Revelation 14:13 we read that Christ's death "was a testimony of God's abhorrence sufficient for the greatest wickedness that ever was in the world that Christ the eternal Son died for it." Grotius could not have stated his governmental theory better.

Yet this Edwardsean assertion is not at the expense of the satisfaction theory. Rather, it is founded on it. True, the manifestation of God's abhorrence of sin is as essential for Edwards as for Grotius. The difference is that for Grotius the manifestation is enough. For Edwards, it is not only not enough but is nothing at all apart from the satisfaction for sin on which its reality as a manifestation of divine abhorrence depends.

SEVEN
REGENERATION

Effectual calling, conversion, repentance, and *regeneration* were approximately synonymous terms for Edwards. An important statement in *Original Sin* shows the identity of the last three terms.

> I put repentance and conversion together, as the Scripture puts them together, Acts iii. 19, and because they plainly signify much the same thing. The word *metanoia* (repentance) signifies a change of the mind; as the word *conversion* means a change or turning from sin to God. And that this is the same change with that which is called *regeneration* (excepting that this latter term especially signifies the change, as the mind is *passive* in it), the following things do show. . . .[1]

This is a rather unfortunate and unscientific way of proceeding. While it is true that Scripture tends to use these different terms synonymously, there are significant differences. Edwards himself notes that the mind, active in repentance, is passive in regeneration. Edwards often notes that *conversion* too has reference to the passivity of the mind as well as its reflex activity. He especially observes that repentance is a change of the mind, which we shall soon see he constantly attributes exclusively to God, the mind of man being passive (if not hostile) at the time of the change. Man's active turning away from sin and toward God is, again, a reflex of God's activity in changing. So, in Edwards, regeneration, repentance, conversion, and effectual calling possess this feature of passivity, though they are all followed by a human response, of course.

THE SINNER IS PASSIVE IN REGENERATION

Regeneration or "efficacious grace" itself is characteristically decisive, immediate, and solely supernatural. This is the main difference between Calvinists (who affirm it) and Arminians (who deny it).

A favorite term in eighteenth-century theology was *physical regeneration,* meaning that the influence of the Holy Spirit in regeneration consists in infusing a new nature *(phusis)* and not merely a moral influence on the old nature.[2] Daniel Whitby, the Arminian, also speaks of the Spirit's work as "physical," but it is clear that he construes physical regeneration as merely a natural effect.[3]

If ever men are turned, God must turn them.[4] God in his Word is especially insistent on this.[5] "I know of no one thing in Scripture wherein such significant, strong expressions are used, in so great variety, or one-half so often, as the testament of this benefit of true goodness and piety of heart."[6] "If God be not the proper bestower, author, and efficient cause of virtue, then the greatest benefits flow not from him; are not owing to his goodness, nor have we him to thank for them."[7] In fact, "There is more of God in it than in almost any other work."[8] If God is stronger than the world, how else could he be so? Ephesians 2:5-10 spells out the divine character of grace: We are saved by grace; grace is God's gift;

we are, therefore, his workmanship; and we were fore-ordained to it. "I know not what the apostle could have said more."[9] Metaphorically, this truth is stated in Romans 7:14: There is no lawful principle in us before we are married to Christ any more than in a remarried woman whose husband still lives.[10] Again, metaphorically speaking, "In saving conversion they that are blind and in darkness have their eyes opened and are turned from darkness unto light."[11] This grace is impossible with men but possible with God, who is able to overcome all resistance.[12]

THE SAINT IS ACTIVE AFTER REGENERATION

At the same time, Edwards is equally insistent on the saints' reflex activity resulting from regeneration or efficacious grace. He calls on the converted to live the converted life.[13] "In efficacious grace," he explains in his treatise, "we are not merely passive, nor yet does God do some, and we do the rest. But God does all and we do all. God produces all, and we act all. For that is what he produces: our own acts. God is the only proper author and fountain; we only are the proper actors. We are, in this respect, wholly passive and wholly active."[14]

Efficacious grace as the gift of God is quite consistent with vigorous activity. Titus was forward in his concern for the saints because God put it in his heart.[15] The human soul voluntarily determines to do good, but this is what the influence of God's Spirit determines.[16]

One of Edwards' most comprehensive and clear descriptions of efficacious grace occurs in his sermon on Romans 2:10:

> Indeed the saints in themselves have no excellence as they are in and of themselves. . . . They are in themselves filthy, vile creatures

and see themselves to be so. But they have an excellence and a glory in them because they have Christ dwelling in them. . . . 'Tis something of God. This holy heavenly spark is put into the soul in conversion, and God maintains it there. All the power of hell cannot put it out. . . . Though it be small . . . 'tis a powerful thing. It has influence on the heart to govern that, and brings forth holy fruits in the life, and won't cease to prevail 'til it has consumed all the corruption that is left in the heart and 'til it has turned the whole soul, as it were, into a pure, holy and heavenly flame.

The principle, once born, grows: "In conversion this spiritual principle begins again to be restored, though it be but in an imperfect degree . . . gets more and more powerful. The house of David waxes stronger and stronger and the house of Saul weaker and weaker."[17] Again, like infants in the womb, all parts of the person are present from the beginning.[18] Conversion is a universal change, as this principle affects all of life, including the body.[19] Conversion is sometimes seen as act, sometimes as process; but it is apparent that Edwards is not lapsing into Arminianism but is thinking of each new act of sanctification as a veritably new moral creation.

Probably the reason Edwards will not let go of the active character of this principle is that he dreads anyone thinking of it in an antinomian fashion. (According to the antinomians, the law was of little or no value for the man of faith. Thus the sanctified life lived under the law is not necessarily authentic evidence for justification. Edwards and other Calvinists reacted against this, of course, claiming that a converted man can and must perform good works as a manifestation of faith.) In his sermon on Deuteronomy 5:27 he says that there is "nothing in heaven or on earth of a more active nature" than the converted man's good works. "Godliness in the heart has a relation to practice as much as a fount has a relation to streams." Grace is "infused." It is this infused principle which makes actions right and not actions that make the principle right (as the Arminians erringly suppose). Likewise, regeneration is the result of predestination: "Conversion or efficacious calling . . . in this the decree begins to bring forth with regard to elect persons."[20]

Consequently, "there is a great difference between converted and unconverted men."[21] First, there is a vast difference in understanding. The unconverted hear about holiness but "see" no excellency in it as the converted do. Second, the unconverted lack conviction of the reality of spiritual things. They are unpersuaded, aware only of problems but unwilling and unable to grasp the solution. Third, unlike the converted, they have no love for God or any desire for any of his qualities. These are real differences because only through spiritual knowledge is one "assimilated" to God. Fourth, relational differences between converted and unconverted are also indicated: union with Christ; freedom from guilt; removal from divine wrath. Fifth, these vast differences which obtain between converted and unconverted argue the necessity also of their ultimate separation.[22]

IRRESISTIBLE GRACE

We noted Edwards' preference for the term *efficacious grace*, but how did he feel about the expression *irresistible grace*?

"The dispute about grace's being resistible or irresistible," he remarks, "is perfect nonsense."[23] The reason is that this grace produces new life and will; therefore, asking whether it is resistible or irresistible is tantamount to asking whether the will opposes the will. If this grace is thought of as enlightening the understanding, then it could be resistible. That would mean that the mind sees so well that it could will it or nil it. If it is objected that the person can still "will what he pleases," this is simply saying that he can will what he wills, which is rather obvious. But, the objection continues, could he not have willed otherwise? Yes, comes Edwards' answer, *if* he had willed otherwise. The whole dispute is nonsense because it only says that man can do what he can do.

REGENERATION ACCORDING TO THE ARMINIANS

"The Arminians found effectual calling to be indecisive, gradual, and natural."[24] This is the assistance of the Holy Spirit, which is a certain meekness or teachability that is not conversion, but leads to conversion.[25] This is the "drawing of the Father." Thus a good and honest heart is the fruit of the Spirit's assistance before actual obedience.

Edwards remarks of this interpretation that Arminianism "comes to the ground."[26] This cryptic comment seems to mean either that the Arminian is here capitulating by seeing "preventing grace" as actual grace (thus taking the Reformed view) or that it conceives of virtue existing before virtue exists (thus contradicting itself). In the same vein, Arminianism construes "becoming as little children" as prior to efficacious graciousness.[27] The new birth is entrance into the kingdom of God,[28] but it comes about by nurture and culture.[29] What it all comes down to, as the Arminian Daniel Whitby puts it, is that efficacious grace amounts to God's giving motives to obedience and virtue.[30] George Turnbull (1698–1748), a Scottish philosopher, likewise thinks that "sudden conversions" in apostolic days were miraculous.[31] But miracles, according to Turnbull and Bishop Butler, are only natural phenomena operating according to unknown laws, which means that angels could affect conversion and God would be unnecessary.[32]

Edwards' critique of the Arminian view of conversion is many-splendored:

1. Nature cannot change nature; only super-nature can (John 3:10).

2. In the Arminian view, God can do no more than the Devil,[33] angels,[34] the Pharisees,[35] and obviously men themselves; only the meaner parts of the process are allotted to God,[36] who can only sow while the Arminians give the increase.[37] God who, according to Scripture, is absolute, sole, and sovereign in this work, is really left out of it.[38]

3. The Arminians have yet to show how righteousness can come to the souls of men without a truly "physical" work of the Holy Spirit.[39]

4. If this work depends on the sinner then, as Stebbing admits, the work may fail to occur.[40]

5. If it were imagined thus to occur, it would mean that man who came into grace on his own could fall out of it the same way.[41]

6. Repentance is specifically called a sovereign gift of God.[42]

7. Paul, the classic case of conversion, was surely not gradually changed.[43]

8. Apostates,[44] who "went out from us" (like Simon the sorcerer)[45] on these principles were still in a converted state.

9. Edwards deals with the favorite illustration of Arminians — the begger accepting alms — by noting that the disposition to receive the proferred gift is the point at issue.[46]

10. If being born again means being admitted to the kingdom, then John 3:5 means that unless a man is born again he cannot enter the kingdom.

Many of the Edwardsean arguments rest on one fundamental principle, fully developed in the *Freedom of the Will* and stated in *Efficacious Grace* in briefer form. The principle is this: Virtuous acts can only come from a disposition to virtue. On Arminian principles they come from nothing, because sinful man has no such disposition.[47] If, on the other hand, Arminians assume that man has a good heart before he comes to Christ in order to be accepted by Christ, then Christ is really unnecessary. If the demands of the law must be reduced to man the sinner's ability to meet them, then why did Christ have to die for sins they were unable to avoid? Actually Arminians have no conception of a good (or evil) heart, because each volition is spontaneously generated apart from any inclination which would destroy a free volition. Consequently, Arminianism comes to oppose the teaching of Scripture because of an underlying false metaphysic, tacitly assumed.

EIGHT
JUSTIFICATION

Articulus stantis aut cadentis ecclesiae ("the doctrine by which the church stands or falls") — so said Martin Luther about justification by faith alone. John Calvin agreed, calling justification by faith the "hinge" of the Reformation. But was that the historic Christian view?

One may say generally of the history of the doctrine of justification that *solafideanism* (justification-by-faith-alone-ism) was taught implicitly, but not explicitly, from the beginning of the church. That is, it was known in the early church that salvation was by faith alone, but not until the sixteenth century was the church called upon to define that teaching more precisely. Those in the church who had quietly apostasized opposed this essential truth (adherents of Tridentine Roman Catholicism), while the faithful (Protestants) affirmed it. The Reformers defined and refined the doctrine in the fires of controversy.

The historian of doctrine, Louis Berkhof, correctly observed that in the early church faith "was generally regarded as the outstanding instrument for the reception of the merits of Christ, and was often called the sole means of salvation."[1] Faith rather than works was "repeatedly expressed by the Apostolic Fathers, and reoccur[s] in the Apologists."[2]

The most influential theologian of the early church was certainly Augustine (354–430). Before we consider his teaching about our crucial doctrine, we note in passing that the standard creed of the Reformation, the Augsburg Confession (1530), found solafideanism in Augustine's mentor and predecessor, Ambrose, under whose preaching Augustine was converted. Article VI of the Confession speaks of solafideanism: "The same [justification by faith] is also taught by the Fathers: For Ambrose says, 'It is ordained of God that he who believes in Christ is saved freely receiving.' "

In spite of this, many cannot find the doctrine in Augustine. Many historical theologians interpret him as confusing justification with sanctification, of which justification is merely a part.[3] This is not accurate, however. Though Augustine finds justification and sanctification inseparable, they are not indistinguishable. Augustinian justification leads into sanctification, but is not confused with it.

According to Augustine, man's faith in Christ justifies him.[4] Confession of Christ is efficacious for the remission of sins.[5] We are justified by the blood of Christ,[6] and we have no merits which are not the gifts of God.[7] Of course, faith is active through love (*fides quae caritate operatur*), but this does not imply that justification is on the basis of love.

Before we leave Augustine, a relatively recent Roman Catholic work requires attention. Father P. Bergauer's *Der Jakobusbrief bei Augustinus (The Epistle of James According to Augustine)* shows clearly that Luther disagreed not only with the Epistle of James but with Augustine as well.[8] Luther became convinced that James was opposed to Paul's doctrine of justification by faith alone and thus dismissed the epistle as noncanonical. This is well-known, but Bergauer also notes that in so doing, Luther was consciously departing from Augustine as well. We sadly agree with Bergauer that Luther erred with respect to both James and Augustine. Bergauer's work confirms, however, what we will shortly note, that Luther was clearly a solafidean, although without recognizing that James and Augustine were also. The Reformer erred, apparently because he could not find explicit forensic language in either James or Augustine.

Ian Sellers sees that it is the post-Augustinian movement which "conflates the immediacy of the act of justification with the later process of sanctification."[9] Nevertheless, many post-Augustinians kept their concepts clear as we will see even in the Scholastic era, though many did not.

Some Roman Catholics like to cry "Forward to the Middle Ages," thinking that they there find authority for their antisolafidean doctrine. But Adolf Harnack insisted that if the medieval church had followed its favorite teacher, Thomas Aquinas, on justification, the Reformation would not have been necessary. The great earlier Scholastic theologian, Anselm, was also solafidean. He wrote his belief in a tract for the consolation of the dying, quoted here by A. H. Strong!

"Question. Dost thou believe that the Lord Jesus died for thee? Answer. I believe it. Qu. Dost thou thank him for his passion and death? Ans. I do thank him. Qu. Dost thou believe that thou canst not be saved except by his death? Ans. I believe it." And then Anselm addresses the dying man: "Come then, while life remaineth in thee: in his death alone place thy whole trust; in naught else place any trust; to his death commit thyself wholly; with this alone cover thyself wholly; and if the Lord thy God will to judge thee, say, 'Lord, between thy judgment and me I present the death of our Lord Jesus Christ; no otherwise can I contend with thee.' And if he shall say that thou art a sinner, say thou: 'Lord, I interpose the death of our Lord Jesus Christ between my sins and thee.' If he say that thou hast deserved condemnation, say: 'Lord, I set the death of our Lord Jesus Christ between my evil deserts and thee, and his merits I offer for those which I ought to have and have not.' If he say that he is wroth with thee, say: 'Lord, I oppose the death of our Lord Jesus Christ between thy wrath and me.' And when thou hast completed this, say again: 'Lord, I set the death of our Lord Jesus Christ between thee and me.'" See Anselm, Opera (Migne), 1:686, 687. The above quotation gives us reason to believe that the New Testament doctrine of justification by faith was implicitly, if not explicitly, held by many pious souls through all the ages of papal darkness.[10]

Thus medieval Scholastics still taught justification as an instantaneous act. It was not until the Council of Trent (1545–1563) that justification was officially confirmed as a process based on human merit derived through divine grace. This was the article—Session VI, Canon 7 of the Council of Trent—which led the Roman Catholic Church away from the orthodox teaching on justification.

For Luther, Romans 1:17 and Matthew 4:7 taught that the righteousness of God was his mercy and pardon. Out went all human merit from indulgences to works of supererogation. As Article IV of Melanchthon's Augsburg Confession, of which Luther approved, phrased it: "Men can be justified freely on account of Christ through faith, when they believe that they are received into grace and that their sins are remitted on account of Christ who made satisfaction for sins on our behalf by his death. God imputes this faith for righteousness in his own sight." Luther elsewhere affirms that Christ's righteousness is ours and our sins are his. Thus, he who was innocent became guilty of depravity, while we who were depraved became innocent.

Calvin, in his *Institutes* (3:11, 15, 20, 27), citing Augustine and Peter Lombard, taught the same doctrine. Though the Genevan saw union with Christ preceding faith (whereas for Luther it *followed* faith), Berkhof is justified in saying "however Calvin may have differed from Luther as to the order of salvation, he quite agreed with him in the nature and importance of the doctrine of justification by faith."[11] Yet Edward Boehl (1836–1903) is correct that Calvin avoided basing justification on the mystical union which equalled intercourse with God. However, this does not justify Boehl in saying that later Reformed theologians did so identify and thus approached the Lutheran heretic, Osiander.[12] (Osiander held to a belief in "essential righteousness," where the Reformed tradition never deviated from the doctrine of "imputed righteousness.")

Nevertheless, John Tillotson, Samuel Clarke, and some other Anglicans did introduce Tridentine thinking into the Church of England by confusing the inseparability of faith and works with the meritoriousness of each.

This same tension toward meritorious righteousness in and by the justified threatened Puritanism from the beginning. That Anglican John Donne (1573–1631) and Congregationalist John Owen (1616–1683), champions of solafideanism, admitted infused righteousness while denying any merit in it shows their sensitivity to the problem. Christopher Fitzsimmons Allison, in *The Rise of Moralism*, traced this English development into Arminianism and beyond in a somewhat parallel way to Joseph Haroutunian's American sketch in *Piety Versus Moralism*.[13]

Puritanism could admit—in fact, insist upon—sanctification (infused righteousness) as strenuously as imputed righteousness. It was inseparably connected with it. The one thing sanctification did not do, for the Puritans, was supplant justification. As we saw, Owen did not even hesitate to speak of *justitia inhaerens*. Righteousness was wrought in a man because it was first imputed to him. The evidence that it was imputed to him was its being wrought in him.

There is a sense in which Puritans saw righteousness as being wrought-in before being imputed-to. This was the prior union with Christ as the psychological basis of justification. "The foundation of imputation is union. Christ and believers actually coalesce into one mystical person."

How did Arminianism emerge out of solafideanism? What was the solafidean offense that led to the departure?

The offense which some found in solafideanism was that it taught acceptance by faith *only*. If this is so, the Arminians argued, an unsanctified man could go to heaven, and that could never be. They were partly right, since an unsanctified man can never go to heaven. But they were partly wrong, for one justified by faith alone is not justified by the faith that is alone. Faith is inseparably connected with works, or sanctification, or inherent righteousness.

Once again, the error was in a failure to understand the truth. A correct objection was based on an incorrect apprehension. How often had the Reformers proclaimed with James (and Paul) that faith without works was dead. Justification without sanctification did not exist. As we have seen, solafideans were not opposed to inherent righteousness except as a *justifying* righteousness, which was precisely what Rome claimed it to be. The orthodox were as opposed—more opposed—to Antinomianism than the unorthodox.

Not understanding that solafideanism gave works a proper role, the Arminians found an improper role for them. Since works, they felt, had to justify—and sinners had none—they used faith to bring down works to a sinner's level. That is, they saw the work of Christ as satisfying God with the imperfect works of men. "Christ brought down the market," according to Richard Baxter.[14] Our inadequate righteousness was made acceptable through Christ.[15] Allison says that this was the imputation of faith of Baxter, Goodwin, and Woodbridge versus the imputation of Christ's righteousness of Owen, Eades, Gataker, Walker, and also of the early Anglicans Hooker, Andrewes, Downame, Davenant, Donne, Ussher, and Hill.[16] Commenting on Arminianism, A. H. Strong has agreed with other scholars that the "Wesleyan scheme is inclined to make faith a work. . . . This is to make faith *the* cause and ground, or at least to add it to Christ's work as a *joint* cause and ground, of justification; . . ."[17]

This, however, is a rather infelicitous way of expressing the difference. It amounts to a pun on the word *impute*. The imputation of Christ's righteousness construes imputation as a reckoning of, or accrediting to, Christ's righteousness. The imputation of faith in this contrast means regarding faith as acceptable which, by legal definition, it is not. Even the Arminians admitted that it was not really acceptable to God (as Christ's righteousness was); but the Son twisted his Father's arm to make him act as if it were. This soteriological perversion was called neonomianism (new-law-ism) because it was not the perfect law of God which was maintained but a new, stepped-down, imperfect, "lawless" law of God. So it became a lapse into justification by works which were not even works.

EDWARDS ON JUSTIFICATION

This was the Arminian import from England that was becoming fashionable in the colonies, much to the distress of the solafidean pastor of Northampton. He had already warned Boston about it in 1731: "Those doctrines and schemes of divinity that are in any respect opposite to such an absolute and universal dependence of God, do derogate from God's glory, and thwart the design of the contrivances for our redemption."[18] In 1734 he felt constrained to bring the matter home to his own people in Northampton with his lectures on justification by faith alone.

The Nature of Justification. For Edwards, justification means being free of guilt and having a righteousness entitling to eternal life. This is made plain at the very beginning of the dual lecture on Romans 4:5.[19] Commenting on Romans

8:29, Edwards says: "In justification are two things, viz, the pardon of sins through Christ's satisfaction and being accepted through his obedience."[20]

We become "free of guilt" by receiving "pardon." Nevertheless, justification does not consist only of pardon, but, says Edwards in Miscellany 812:

> It does not in strictness consist at all in pardon of sin but in an act or sentence approving of him as innocent and positively righteous and so having a right to freedom from punishment and to the reward of positive righteousness. Pardon as the word is used in other cases signifies a forgiving one freely though he is not innocent or has no right to be looked on as such. There is nothing of his own he has to offer that is equivalent to innocence, but he justly stands guilty; but notwithstanding his guilt he is freed from punishment. But the pardon we have by Christ is a freeing persons from punishment of sin as an act of justice and because they are looked upon and accepted as having that which is equivalent to innocence. . . .
>
> Justification consists in imputing righteousness. To pardon sin is to cease to be angry for sin. But imputing righteousness and ceasing to be angry are two things. One is the foundation of the other. God ceases to be angry with the sinner for his sin because righteousness is imputed to him. . . .
>
> Persons cannot be justified without a righteousness consistent with God's truth for it would be a false sentence. It would be to give sentence concerning a person that he is approvable as just that is not just and cannot be approved as such in a true judgment. To suppose a sinner pardoned without a righteousness implies no contradiction, but to justify without a righteousness is self-contradictory.

Righteousness. Though the definition of justification is more comprehensive, the actual doctrine of the sermons on Romans 4:5 is that "we are justified only by faith in Christ, and not by any manner of virtue or goodness of our own."[21] This is, of course, the tenor of the text used: "Now to him that worketh not, but believeth on him that justifieth the ungodly, his faith is counted for righteousness." The contrast in Edwards' statement is between "faith in Christ" and "virtue or goodness of our own." As Edwards develops the concept, however, the contrast is not between our faith and our goodness but between Christ's goodness and our non-goodness. Referring to our faith is a shorthand way of referring to Christ's righteousness, which is crucial. The "merit" is Christ's.[22]

In a later sermon on Romans 4:16, Edwards seems to reduce justification to righteousness, but a "twofold righteousness": "Nothing else seems to be intended by it in the New Testament than a person's being looked upon by God as having a righteousness belonging to him and God accordingly judging of it meet that he should be dealt with as such."[23] This twofold righteousness consists of freedom from guilt which the First Adam enjoyed — and actual fulfillment of a law — which only the Second Adam achieved. This righteousness may be performed by the person himself as the First Adam was supposed to do and the elect angels did. Or it could be by "some other person who has performed it for him whose act God sees meet to accept for him, as fallen men are justified."[24]

This is important to Edwards because he sees no way of justification for a person except by righteousness. "Works are the fixed price of eternal life; it is fixed by an eternal unalterable rule of righteousness."[25] There cannot be justification without righteousness. Edwards solemnly reiterates the Reformed emphasis on righteousness in justification by faith alone. God justifies the "ungodly"[26] to be sure, but Edwards carefully explains this: "We must indeed be saved on the account of works; but not our own. It is on account of the works which Christ hath done for us."[27]

In the sermon on Matthew 7:21, Edwards puts the matter plainly: "God acting the part of a judge determines and declares that men have a righteousness and as they are justified by works."[28]

The Romans 4:5 sermon gives us the rationale of imputed righteousness:

> While God beholds man from Christ, he must behold him as he is in himself; and so his goodness cannot be beheld by God, but as taken with his guilt and hatefulness; and as put in the scales with it; and being beheld so, his goodness is nothing; because there is a finite on the balance versus an infinite, whose proportion to it is nothing.
>
> Though a respect to that natural suitableness between such a qualification, and such a state, does go before justification, yet the acceptance even of faith as any goodness or loveliness of the believer, follows justification. . . .
>
> But to suppose that God gives a man an interest in Christ in reward for his righteousness or virtue is inconsistent with his still remaining under condemnation 'til he has an interest in Christ. . . .[29]

The Basis of Justification. So justification is righteousness, however we come by it. We do not come by it by ourselves, but by Christ. *How* we come by it by Christ is the question.

Edwards' answer is clear: Christ's righteousness belongs to the faithful by virtue of their "natural union" with him. The Reformers, especially Calvin, and the Puritans, especially Owen, also saw union with Christ as the basis of justification. Edwards is, perhaps, even more precise in two ways: First, he observes that Christ achieves his own righteousness which, second, becomes ours by union with him. Christ "was not justified 'til he had done the work the Father had appointed him, and kept the Father's commandments through all the trials: and then in his resurrection he was justified,"[30] And in him we are justified because of the "natural fitness" of those united to him possessing what he achieved for them.

> When it is said that we are not justified by any righteousness or goodness of our own, what is meant is, that it is not out of respect to the excellency or goodness of any qualifications or acts in us whatsoever, that God judges it meet that this benefit of Christ should be

ours and it is not in any wise, on account of any excellency or value that there is in faith, that it appears in the sight of God a meet thing, that he that believes should have this benefit of Christ assigned to him, but purely from the relation faith has to the person in which this benefit is to be had, or as it unites to that mediator, in and by whom we are justified.[31]

Before a person believes, he is not possessed of this congruity.[32]

At this point Edwards goes further than his predecessors by distinguishing between a "twofold fitness,"[33] which he calls natural and moral. He affirms the first and denies the second as belonging to the believer. The second is denied because, he reasons, it would imply an "amiableness" in the believer's faith which it does not possess. A "natural suitableness" is always included in a "moral," but natural suitableness "by no means necessarily includes a moral."[34]

The Means of Justification. If natural fitness or congruity is the basis of justification, the Edwardsean means to it is faith, faith alone and uniquely. This is very clear in the addresses on Romans 4:5. It is brilliantly exhibited in the later sermon on Romans 4:16, "That the grace of God in the new covenant eminently appears in this, that it proposes justification by faith."[35] Faith, according to Miscellany 1280, is not really a "condition" because Christ is the "ultimate condition" and besides, there are other "conditions."[36] "Faith is that in them which God has regard to upon the account of which God judges it meet that they should be looked upon as having Christ's righteousness belonging to 'em . . . upon the account of which God in his wisdom sees it proper that they should have an actual communion with Christ in his righteousness." Continuing, he states that "tho we can't be justified without other graces and shall be justified with them yet we are not justified by 'em because they are not what God has regard to upon the account of which he judges it proper that men should be looked upon as being in Christ and so having an interest in his righteousness."[37] Nor are we justified by faith considered as a work ("by virtue of the goodness or loveliness of it").

As with Luther and others, the marriage analogy was a favorite of Edwards.

> As when a man offers himself to a woman in marriage; he doesn't give himself to her as a reward of her receiving him in marriage: Her receiving him is not considered as a worthy deed in her, for which he rewards her, by giving himself to her; but 'tis by her receiving him, that the union is made, by which she hath him for her husband: 'Tis on her part the unition it self. The woman, by virtue of her natural union with the husband as one flesh, becomes also the possessor of all that belongs to the man: his position, wealth, and the like. So with the believer: by his natural union with Christ by the Spirit he becomes the possessor of all the righteousness of Christ also.[38]

That faith is the means is clearest of all in the later Miscellanies 831, 877, and 1250. Almost the last Miscellany, 1354, is dedicated to this theme.

THE PROOF OF JUSTIFICATION

Granted that Edwards was correct in his analysis of the biblical doctrine of justification, what proof does he offer that it was true? For Edwards, such a question was impertinent. The Bible is the Word of God. What it teaches, God teaches. Against the deists, Edwards argued that each proposition of revelation did not have to be separately demonstrated any more than each proposition of sense or history had to be separately proven.[39]

In the sermon on Romans 4:20 he discusses Abraham's faith as he had elucidated the faith of saints in general in his exposition of Habakkuk 2:4.[40] The theme of this very early sermon is "That saints do live by faith."[41] The young preacher defined faith as the soul's acquiescing in the divine sufficiency, specifically the sufficiency of Jesus Christ. He then takes up the question of how spiritual life comes by faith. Faith, he says, entitles one to life. If anyone fears the shadow of Catholicism there, Edwards hastens to explain that faith is "that by which the soul is united to Christ." It is Christ alone who entitles to life.

The inspired Word of God everywhere teaches this essential doctrine. Miscellany 725 had many references to the doctrine, even in the Old Testament, even in statements that were cited in evidence against the doctrine. His more famous lectures on Romans 4:5 abound in biblical references for this indispensable doctrine, dealing pointedly with the Roman Catholic claims to the contrary.

CRUCIALITY OF THE DOCTRINE

Thomas A. Schafer observes that Jonathan Edwards said much less about this doctrine in his last twenty years.[42] He shifted his focus from this fruit of Arminianism to its root in the libertarian, voluntaristic view of the will. As Edwards concludes in his *Freedom of the Will*, all Reformed doctrines were subverted by the Arminian view of freedom.[43] The third part is entitled: "Wherein Is Inquired, Whether Any Such Liberty of Will as Arminians Hold, Be Necessary to Moral Agency, Virtue and Vice, Praise and Dispraise, etc."[44] In it he proved not only that Arminianism was not necessary to virtue but that it doomed the biblical way of virtue and salvation. As in "Justification by Faith" he saw the Arminian way of salvation with its stress on human righteousness as the end of human and divine virtue.

There can be no doubt that this doctrine was as essential

for Edwards as for Paul and the Reformers. The contrary doctrine, he insists, citing Romans 9 and 10, is "fatal" and "another gospel," according to Galatians 1:6. It is the substitution of man's virtue for Christ's, a legal system for the gospel, the covenant of works for the covenant of grace.

"I am sensible," he concludes, "the divines of that side [Arminianism] entirely disclaim the popish doctrine of *merit* and are free to speak of our utter unworthiness, and the great imperfections of all our services. But after all, they maintain, it is our *virtue,* imperfect as it is, that commends men to God. . . . Whether they allow the term merit or not, we are accepted by our merit in the same sense as the first Adam."[45]

In his discussion of James and Paul, Edwards notes that they were using the word *justify* in different senses, and he insists that we should alter the words there "because there is no one doctrine in the whole Bible more fully asserted."[46]

EDWARDS' CONTRIBUTIONS

Jonathan Edwards made many contributions to the historic doctrine of justification by faith alone. He continued it as the central doctrine of Christianity and American Protestantism, affirming it in *God Glorified in Man's Dependence* (1731), proving it in *Justification by Faith* (1734), establishing its metaphysical foundation in *Freedom of the Will* (1754), and expounding it in numerous published and unpublished sermons.

He connected it inseparably with the covenant of grace, showing that covenant theology, so far from being "incipient Arminianism," was the antithesis of it. In fact, he demonstrated that Arminianism was founded on a covenant of works mentality, and was essentially a denial of the gospel and purely gracious salvation.

In line with Calvin and Puritanism he saw union with Christ as the grounds of justification. And going beyond his own tradition he developed "fitness," or natural congruity, as the corollary of union with Christ, sharply contrasting it with any "moral fitness" in faith or obedience.

More sharply than any he saw the sense in which justification by faith alone rested ultimately on justification by works — the works of Christ. He showed that faith justified works rather than works justifying faith. "Rewards" were explained thoroughly in solafidean terms, while he annihilated any concept of merit anywhere except in Jesus Christ.

He made the doctrine of justification the centerpiece in evangelism. God himself confirmed this doctrine by a great awakening following its preaching. Edwards' prelude to his most celebrated evangelistic proclamation of "Justification by Faith Alone" cites this:

> The following discourse of justification, that was preached (though not so fully as it is here printed) at two *public lectures*, seemed to be remarkably blessed, not only to establish the judgments of many in this truth, but to engage their hearts in a more earnest pursuit of justification, in that way that had been explained and defended; and *at that time,* when I was greatly reproached for defending this doctrine in the pulpit, and just upon my suffering a very open abuse for it, God's work wonderfully brake forth amongst us, and souls began to flock to Christ, as the Saviour in whose righteousness alone they hoped to be justified. So that this was the doctrine on which this work in its beginning was founded, as it evidently was in the whole progress of it.[47]

NINE
SANCTIFICATION

PURITANISM, EDWARDS, AND SANCTIFICATION

In the twelve-hundred-plus sermons that Edwards wrote, sanctification was probably the central and most emphasized theme. Edwards is famous, of course, for the imprecatory sermons which were designed mainly to awaken persons to consider the spiritual life, but the delineation of that life occupied Edwards far more.

Not only the sermons but lectures as well were preoccupied with this theme. Most famous are those contained in the *Treatise on Religious Affections* (1746), but the first published series on justification opposed both antinomianism and neonomianism in its insistence on a sound doctrine of sanctification as a corollary of justification. *A Faithful Narrative of the Surprising Work of God* (1736) followed by the *Thoughts on Revival* (1742) pursued that theme determinedly. What was the *Humble Attempt* but a call to a life of prayer? One of the avowed principles in *Freedom of the Will* was to preserve the Reformed gospel of grace. Not only the late *Nature of True Virtue* treats sanctification but even *The End for Which God Created the World* sees remanation, return to God, as the goal of all God's redemptive activity.

In emphasizing sanctification, Edwards was in the mainstream of the Puritan tradition. William Haller has noted that theologian-historian Ernst Troeltsch and sociologist Max Weber have exaggerated the speculative aspects of the theology of the Puritans, who were actually more activistic and practical than theoretical. Indeed, in refuting Troeltsch and Weber, Haller jumps to the erroneous conclusion that the Puritans were actually Arminian. It is true that "Puritan sermons before the revolution were chiefly concerned with charting in infinite detail and tireless reiteration the course of the godly soul out of hardness and indifference to the consciousness of its lost condition, and so out of despair and repentance to faith in God, to active perseverance and confident expectation of victory and glory."[1] The Puritans were not Arminians, but they were greatly concerned with growing steadily in faith and good works.

The Puritan Richard Sibbes had written that "where true grace is, it groweth in measure and purity. Smoking flax will grow to a flame."[2] A. V. G. Allen has noted the same emphases in Jonathan Edwards, going so far as to say that "God is in the process of delivering from sin."[3]

Sanctification consists in good works which must be "universal." "A true trust in Christ is never infused without other graces with it."[4] This is the reason Edwards could preach that a pretense of trusting Christ is in vain as long as men live wicked lives. Faith rules out such a life, for it infuses the virtues with itself. It aims at virtue as such and therefore at universal virtue. If there were any virtue that it did not love, it could not be said to aim at virtue as such but only some particular virtues, and these would be cultivated for some reason other than themselves; for, if they were cultivated for themselves alone, all virtue would be cultivated. "The graces are so related one to another that one includes and infers another."[5]

EXACTLY

THE NECESSITY OF SANCTIFICATION

As we have seen, justification is by faith alone, but not by the faith that is alone. It is impossible that men should be saved without an evangelical, universal, and sincere obedience under the second covenant. Obedience is as necessary now as it was under the old covenant of works, though not for the same reason.[6] In the old covenant life was to be obtained on the basis of man's works. This is not so in the new covenant. Nevertheless, in the new covenant works are the necessary evidence of the genuineness of the faith by which alone men are justified.

Granted that it is necessary that a man be holy if he would see the Lord and possess eternal life, the question arises as to *why* it is necessary. It is because God says so; but the question still remains: Why does God say so? This question appealed to the searching mind of Edwards, and from his earliest preaching we have important sermons on the subject. For example, in his 1733 sermon on Hebrews 12:14, Edwards says: "None will ever be admitted to see Christ but only holy persons."[7] A major part of the sermon is devoted to the reasons for this doctrine. But we shall consider more particularly another early sermon, on Isaiah 35:8. Its doctrine is: "Those only that are holy are in the way to heaven."[8] In this message holiness is defined as conformity of the heart, not merely outward conformity to God's holy law.

The reasons that Edwards here gives for the necessity of holiness are four in number. First, it is contrary to reason to make the wicked equally happy with the holy. Justice obliges God to punish sin (Exod. 34:3; Num. 14:18).

Second, a holy God cannot embrace a filthy creature. "It is therefore as impossible for an unholy thing to be admitted unto the happiness of heaven as it is for God not to be, or be turned to nothing."[9] It is impossible for God to love sin or to love complacently a wicked man. "It is as impossible that

God should love sin as it is for him to cease to be, and it is as impossible for him to love a wicked man that has not his sin purified. And it is as impossible for him to enjoy the happiness of heaven except God love him, for the happiness of heaven consists in the enjoyment of God's love."[10] Edwards is here, no doubt, speaking of a love of complacency, not of benevolence. He makes the above statement more than once, but he does not often take the time to explain the different uses of the word *love,* though it is clear from his many utterances that he represents God as having a love of benevolence for the wicked and ungrateful. For example, the doctrine of the sermon on Luke 6:35 is: "God is kind to the unthankful and to the evil."[11]

Third, God could not only not love filthy creatures, but such a love would defile both him and heaven. It would fill heaven with the "loathsome stench of sin."[12]

Fourth, there is a reason inherent in the nature of sin which makes it necessary that the sinner be unhappy and incapable of being happy. That is, sin is a cruel tyrant, necessarily involving the soul defiled by it in misery. In its very nature it is rebellion and confusion; it could not coexist with happiness. It is, therefore, impossible that an unholy person should be happy or inherit heaven. By the same token, holiness is necessary to glory. In a later sermon Edwards gives six reasons for the necessity of holiness for happiness.[13]

SANCTIFICATION AS EVIDENCE OF GRACE

Good works are not only necessary but they are very convincing demonstrations of the reality of a Christian's experience. For one thing, when Satan sees them he knows that he has been defeated and that one of his former captives is his no more. "When the professors of religion walk according to their profession, God is so exalted by it that he thereby ob-

tains a glorious triumph over the devil."[14] It is not profession that convinces Satan, but practical holiness alone. Such
actual holiness is convincing to men as well as devils. "A
manifestation of godliness in a man's life and walk is a better
ground of other's charity concerning his godliness, than any
account that he gives about it in words."[15] It runs as a refrain
through Edwards' preaching that actions speak louder than
words. Indeed, the greatest test of religious experience (with
respect to others and to oneself) in his most famous treatise
on the subject, *Religious Affections,* is clearly this one.[16] One
of the deepest discussions of the holiness of the believer is
found in the sermon on Psalm 119:3.[17] The doctrine of this
sermon is "The spirit that godly men are of is a spirit to be
perfectly holy."

Edwards observes that a Christian is never satisfied with
anything less than being perfectly holy. For him, any remaining sin is a great burden and he will not be fully happy until
it is removed. He does not "allow" any sin, but on the contrary
fights against all remaining sin relentlessly. He will not neglect any known duty, for he is opposed to sins of omission as
of commission. He will make an effort, not to know as little
as possible of his duty, but as much as possible, and will come
as close to perfection as it is possible in his present state. He
loves the law, and that not in spite of its strictness but because
of it.

In the sermon on Psalm 139:23, 24, Edwards compares the
witness of a godly life with the power of preaching: "If those
that call themselves Christians generally thus walked in all
the paths of virtue and holiness, it would tend more to the
advancement of the kingdom of Christ in the world, the convincing of sinners and propagating religion among un-
believers than all the sermons in the world, when the lives of
those that are called Christians are as they are."[18]

As far as God, who searches the heart, is concerned,

"There can be no acceptable glory and honor given to God without grace. One truly sincere person gives more glory to God than a whole world of wicked men."[19] Such a person's giving a cup of cold water in the name of Christ means far more to God than an unconverted person giving his body to be burned. Although this grace in the souls of saints is exceedingly small, it is very powerful and, by divine constitution, indestructible. "Christianity consists very much in practice" and not merely in belief in doctrine and the catechism, Edwards preached.[20] It is a "very active thing." It is called a doctrine according to godliness, and it leads to a "laborious" life.[21]

That grace is powerful is the theme of the sermon on 2 Timothy 3:5.[22] This is seen in the very nature of its acting; truely Christians are baptized with fire.

The fact that faith's working is able to mortify the lusts of the human heart is evidence of its power. The natural man cannot mortify his own lusts. All he does is to close one vent and open another so that his lusts, if curtailed in one direction, may continue to express themselves in another. Nor is reason and learning able to mortify lusts. Not even religion can do it if it is without grace. But grace can overcome man's depravity. So we have a view of Christian grace that even in great weakness is greater than the lusts of the depraved human heart.

SANCTIFICATION AS STRUGGLE

While the Christian has a new and powerful principle that overcomes his lusts, these lusts are still present.[23] As noted above, there is more sin than grace in the Christian. The "natural distempers" (apparently he means those patterns of behavior to which some men are especially prone by nature) also obscure the principle of grace, and grace does not always shine clearly through them.[24] Furthermore, even in the saint's most excellent experiences of grace, the evil spirit is prone to inject itself. Edwards says that he has known in an abundance of instances that "the Devil has come in the midst of the most excellent frames,"[25] just as Christ himself was led into the wilderness to be tempted by the Devil immediately after the coming of the Holy Spirit upon him.

The inevitable result of the presence of these two diverse and antagonistic principles in the heart is a bitter struggle. "That inward mutual opposition and strife that there is between grace and corruption in the hearts of the saints during their continuance in this world" is the theme of the sermon on Galatians 5:17, one of Edwards' fullest treatments of it.[26] There is in the godly heart a struggle going on comparable to that which went on in the womb of Rebecca as Jacob sought to supplant Esau.[27] Warfare is another analogy Edwards used to describe the struggle in the heart of the converted person. "In order to our being preserved from destruction by our spiritual enemies we have need to behave ourselves in the business of religion as those that are engaged in the most dangerous war."[28]

The same truth is expressed from another viewpoint in the sermons on Luke 22:32. These sermons assume that the believer will be defeated constantly by his adversary and must continue the battle and replenish his resources by a constant conversion to God. "Those that have true grace in their hearts may yet stand in great need of being converted."[29] There are subsequent changes that the godly undergo which are spoken of in the like terms of the first change, which is commonly called *conversion* (Ps. 51:13; Isa. 6:10; Acts 3:19). The first work of conversion is called a putting off of the old man (Col. 4:22f.). Spiritual resurrection signifies regeneration (Eph. 2:1, 5), but it also means later works (Eph. 1:6). Saints are exhorted to be transformed

(Rom. 12:1). The Corinthian saints were urged to be reconciled to God (2 Cor. 5:20). The disciples must be converted,
according to Christ in Matthew, chapter 18.

SANCTIFICATION AND ASSURANCE OF SALVATION

How does a person know whether his moral defeat is a mark
of reprobation or only a sign of Christian imperfection? In
the application of his sermon on Revelation 17:14[30] Edwards considers this question. The saint may be deceived, he
says, citing Noah, Lot, and Elijah as examples. A faithful man
may be "surprised" and suddenly supplanted, or overtaken.
But it is not the way of a true Christian to fall utterly away under ordinary temptation. If a person does that, he is not
faithful, that is, not converted. "All true saints justify the gospel of Jesus Christ," he says.[31] It would be utterly inconsistent for a faith that arises from a view of the glory of God and
the awfulness of sin not to express itself in consonant works.

"What is religion?" the Puritan sage asks, and answers it
saying: "Nothing else but the creature's exercise and
manifestation of respect to the divine being."[32] Let us not,
he urges in another sermon, trust in any supposed coming to
Christ. Careful examination will easily distinguish between
a mere "flush of affection" and counting the cost and following him.[33] True converts take Christ's yoke upon them. It is a
mark of true revival that there is a drastic alteration in behavior. "When the Spirit of God has been remarkably
poured out on a people, a thorough reformation of those
things that before were amiss amongst them ought to be the
effect of it."[34] When the Spirit is thus come upon men there
is a tendency to three things: awakening, converting, and
confirming. "Some men are reformed that are not converted, but none are converted but what are reformed."[35]

Edwards preached often that very few persons among

those who professed faith and sanctification would be saved. Even among those in Christian countries and making a Christian profession few would be saved. "There are but few even of those that live under the calls of the gospel that shall be saved."[36] In this sermon he observes, in passing, what he preached frequently, that none but those "under the calls of the gospel" ever are saved. (He seems to have excepted some children, for he believed there were elect and saved children.) But even of those who have the benefits of the means of grace and the opportunity of being redeemed, the vast majority perish. In his *Original Sin* he uses this fact as a proof of universal corruption. "Even these means have been ineffectual upon the far greater part of them with whom they have been used; of the many that have been called, few have been chosen."[37] Many Bible passages are cited in support of this doctrine, such as Matthew 22:4, Luke 13:23-24; 1 Corinthians 9:24. We find it typified in Isaiah 10:22 and Jeremiah 2:3. The "remnant" concept in the Old Testament is appealed to, and the people of God are called a "little flock." They are redeemed out of the world; the world itself perishes. Most of those who hope for heaven are on the broad road to destruction.[38] Men are on this broad road because they are blind, but even the blind are able to find that road; indeed, they are born on it.

TEN

THE LATTER-DAY GLORY AND SECOND COMING

The idea of the latter days was a controlling concept in Edwards' thinking. His earliest Miscellanies (especially 26, 158, and 262) make reference to it. During the First Awakening he was discussing it in his preaching (for example, the April 1735 sermon on "Ruth's Resolution"). Between the awakenings, in 1737, long before *The Humble Attempt*, he presented his people with a comprehensive yet urgent message, based on Ecclesiastes 11:2.[1] He told his people that while some are presumptuous in fixing the exact time of the world's end, others err in not being prepared for what is revealed. This much he assured them: These glorious times could not be very far off.

One of his most interesting sermons on this theme is on Isaiah 26:10-11. It is the only sermon on this Isaianic chapter devoted almost entirely to the latter days, and it deals with the destruction of the wicked at the time: "The obstinancy of some wicked men is such that means won't turn them, nor will all the advantages enjoyed in God's visible church make any effect upon them nor will any of God's providential judgments or threatenings reclaim them."[2]

The Great Awakening in Northampton made Edwards

think that the latter days were rapidly approaching. Though his calendar of the Apocalypse did not call for the destruction of the Antichrist until 1866, in his sermon on Matthew 24:35 he indicates he was expecting the overthrow of evil in the world and the national conversion of the Jews.[3]

The British victory over the threatening French at Cape Breton in 1745 was seen as a sign of the end times. After giving a detailed account of the military success, Edwards exclaims: "The whole is wonderful from beginning to end. No parallel in history. We live in a day of wonders. Great reason to think that God is now about to fulfill the prophecies."[4]

Negative and positive "signs" were appearing, parallel to the first Advent. Negative indications (which were common excesses of revivals) included bodily effects, unusual events, noise, wide use of means, irregularities (including errors and delusions as well as counterfeits and scandals).[5] Positive signs included the Spirit's leading souls to Christ, operating against Satan's kingdom, convincing of truth, and promoting love and humility. Those who denied these signs were reminded that the Pharisees did not see the signs of their times either and were rebuked by the Lord; Edwards warned his people against hearkening to these deniers. In his sermon on Isaiah 27:13, Edwards speaks of the possible blowing of the Jubilee trumpet.[6]

Prayer should be poured out for the latter days in which the Spirit "will operate in a remarkable manner as a spirit of prayer."[7] In the Isaiah 62:6 sermon he urges saints to make their election sure by prayer for these days and urges "natural" men to pray for their conversion at that time.[8] Other virtues besides prayer will also appear. "In the future times of the church of God saints shall be like trees that are always green."[9] Love will abound, and glorifying God by word and deed will be characteristic.

THE MILLENNIUM

We have seen how Edwards perceived the nearness and the signs and the necessary prayer preceding the coming of the latter-day glory, but what precisely was to be the nature of this Millennium? One important feature was the saints being recognized in the world; another, that it was the time of Christ's "espousals."

Edwards' comments on the key biblical verse describing the Millennium (Rev. 20:4) and his concept of the meek inheriting the earth are interesting.

First, the Millennium will feature saints being recognized and exalted in this world where they had been so long persecuted. They are recognized in Christ by virtue of their union with him (Miscellany K). No details of this reign are given except that it is long and peaceful, though Satan is not completely overthrown.

Second, this will be the time of Christ's "espousals." "The day of the commencement of the church's latter-day glory is eminently the day of Christ's espousals, when as the bridegroom rejoiceth over the bride, so he will rejoice over his church."[10] So he interprets the wedding of the Lamb in Revelation 14 and 19, though it precedes the description of the beginning of the Millennium in chapter 19.

Edwards nowhere discusses the precise time of the Millennium, but he does state that it is to be taken literally. It is to be a Sabbath rest, meaning, for Edwards, that it is to follow the six thousand years of human history with the appropriate seventh day of rest (one thousand years).[11] If not precisely a thousand years, at least it will be a "very long time."[12] Among other evidences of prosperity and affluence during the Millennium, there will be a population explosion.[13]

His comment on Revelation 20:4 in the Apocalypse Series explains the sense in which "martyrs under Anti-christ, might be said to rise and reign in the time of the Millennium."[14] A later reference in the same series merely asserts that saints do reign in the Millennium.[15]

Though not specifically mentioned in comments on Revelation 20:4, Edwards surely conceived of the Millennium as that period of time when the meek inherit this earth:

> The meek (those that meekly and patiently suffer with Christ, and for his sake) shall inherit the earth: they shall inherit it, and reign on earth with Christ. Christ is the heir of the world; and when the appointed time of his kingdom comes, his inheritance shall be given him, and then the meek, who are joint-heirs, shall inherit the earth. . . . The saints in heaven will be as much with Christ in reigning over the nations, and in the glory of his dominion at that time, as they will be with him in the honour of judging the world at the last day. That promise of Christ to his disciples, Matt. xix. 28, 29, seems to have a special respect to the former of these. In vs. 28 Christ promises to the disciples, that hereafter, when the Son of man shall sit on the throne of his glory, they shall sit on twelve thrones, judging the twelve tribes of Israel.[16]

THE MILLENNIUM AND THE
AMERICAN REVOLUTION

It is somewhat ironic that scholars writing two and a quarter centuries later see in Edwards' millennial thinking a charter for American "manifest destiny." For Edwards, the hope was that America (that is, the colonies) would turn from its evil ways and seek the Lord even more earnestly than in her beginnings.

Whether Edwards would have favored the American Revolution is difficult to determine. We know that he saw the Millennium as a time of liberty. The repudiations of Christianity as the official religion of the new republic could only have grieved him.

In general terms, Edwards conceived of Christ's Second

Coming as following the Millennium. This view was in sharp contrast to eighteenth-century premillennialists who saw it preceding the Millennium.

THE KINGDOM OF GOD

The kingdom of the Christ was at first the kingdom of the Jews, whose Messiah he claimed to be. When they rejected him, the kingdom of Christ was apart from the Jews, since only a few joined. It came then, Edwards says, in four stages. First, Matthew 16:28 indicates its coming in the fall of Jerusalem. Second, the kingdom comes with the fall of the heathen Roman Empire at the advent of Emperor Constantine (Rev. 6). The fall of the Antichrist as described in Daniel 7 and Revelation marks the third stage. Fourth, the fall of all the wicked and establishment of the righteous at the Day of Judgment is the final and perfect form of the kingdom of Christ. Formidable opposition appears at each critical stage: the Jews at the first, heathen and papal Rome at the second and third, Gog and Magog at the fourth. Each stage is a type of the last day, with a "resurrection" occurring at each epoch.[17]

Edwards was persuaded that Christ would conquer both heathenism and Islam before handing over his kingdom to the Father,[18] hence his well-known post-millennialism. H. Richard Niebuhr saw this confidence in the sovereign power of God as what led to Edwards' great millennial expectation and hope.[19]

The climax of the kingdom begins rather than ends at the Day of Judgment. Christ at that time shall deliver up his kingdom to the Father (Miscellany 434). Nevertheless, Christ will continue to reign, but in a different manner. At his Ascension, Christ was invested with kingly glory; at the Day of Judgment he will receive greater glory. At present, and until the Day of Judgment, Christ rules by delegated authority; after the judgment he will rule by virtue of his union with God. Now the Father reigns through his Son; then, with the Son and the saints sitting on Christ's throne, the Father shall reign with both forever (Miscellany 736). Christ will remain Mediator forever; so, the kingdom he delivers up is not his "mediatorial" but his "representative kingdom" (Miscellany 742).

This is Edwards' Note on the Bible No. 158 on 1 Corinthians 15:28:

> 1 Cor. xv. 28. "And when all things shall be subdued unto him, then shall the Son also himself be subject unto him that put all things under him, that God may be all in all." Christ as Mediator has now the kingdom and government of the world so committed to him, that he is to all intents and purposes in the room of his Father. He is to be respected as God himself is, as supreme, and absolute, and sovereign Ruler. God has left the government in his hands wholly, now since his exaltation, that he may himself have the accomplishment and finishing of those great things for which he died. He is made head over all things to the church until the consummation; and he is now king of the church, and of the world, in his present state of exaltation. He is not properly a subordinate ruler, because God hath entirely left the government with him, to his wisdom, and to his power. But after Christ has obtained all the ends of his labours and death, there will be no farther occasion for the government's being after that manner in his hands. He will have obtained by his government, all the ends he desired; and so then God the Father will resume the government, and Christ and his church will spend eternity in mutual enjoyment, and in the joint enjoyment of God; . . . God will be respected as supreme orderer, and Christ with his church united to him, and dependent on him, shall together receive of the benefit of his government.[20]

There are those who say that all this is wishful eschatological thinking that cannot be proven, but Edwards insists the opposite is the case. This eschatological pattern is the only rational possibility and therefore proves Christianity true

(Miscellanies 743, 745, 952). All revolutions of time and history are obviously for the man who understands them. So, man must remain or nothing would come of all these revolutions. All this confirms the Christian revelation that the world is coming to an end and man will continue. Otherwise it would all come "to nothing from which it was made" if "he that is carried in the chariot doesn't remain after he is brought with so much labor and vast ado to the end of his journey, but ceases to be as the chariot itself does."[21]

THE SECOND COMING OF CHRIST

Edwards' devotion to the latter-day glory and the Millennium only increased his zeal for the Second Coming of Jesus Christ. All that preceded, however glorious, was but preparation for and anticipation of that grand event of the eschatological timetable. Even Christ's coming triumphantly on the white horse as depicted in Revelation 19 was but the prelude to the glorious latter days and Millennium. Nothing but the even more glorious Second Coming itself could upstage such splendor.

Though persuaded that Scripture does not allow the calculation of the exact date of the Parousia, Edwards was insistent that it did indicate the general period. The fullest development of this is in an unpublished sermon on John 1:10.[22] The application is especially interesting. The prophecies make us believe, said Edwards in 1741, that the coming of Christ is not far distant. Furthermore, there is reason to believe that Christ's reception, or lack of it, at the Second Coming will parallel his first coming.

What signs, Edwards inquires, will distinguish the return of Christ? Paralleling his procedure in *Religious Affections,* he first enumerates signs that do *not* prove the Second Advent, such as bodily effects, noise, irregularities, delusions, counterfeits, and scandals. Positive indications are the Holy Spirit leading people to Christ, his operation against Satan's kingdom, convincing of truth, and pouring out of the spirit of love and humility. The Devil will try to deceive, to be sure, but there are some things he could not do if he would and some he would not if he could. The sermon concludes abruptly with a warning against the unpardonable sin which opponents risk. To his own people, he says: "I warn against hearkening to them. . . ."[23]

It is rather interesting that this great postmillenniarian, all his great expectations for the future notwithstanding, believed only few would be saved. "This world," he wrote, "is like a sinking ship" (Miscellany 520).

But whenever Christ returns, it will be a great day of rejoicing for the saints. "Christ, at his first coming, came to bear the sins of his people for the procuring of their salvation. At his Second Coming, he will appear without bearing any sins for the bestowment of salvation."[24] That is the reason all saints love Christ's return. At his first coming his glory was under a veil but it is unveiled at the Second Coming as he will be revealed in both his divine and human natures. Therefore, " 'tis the character of true saints to love the appearing of Jesus Christ at the last day,"[25] even though (and especially though) they will probably be suffering persecution when the Parousia occurs. " 'Tis probable many of the saints at that time will be found suffering persecution, for there are several things in Scripture that seem to hold forth that the time when Christ is coming shall be a time when wickedness shall exceedingly abound and the saints be greatly persecuted."[26]

This is a rather surprising way of putting the matter. Elsewhere Edwards had indicated that following the Millennium would be the greatest tribulation the church was ever to know.

A CRITICAL QUESTION
ABOUT THE SECOND COMING

At this point we may notice a critical concern of Edwards. Much scholarship then and now contends that the apostles taught that the Second Coming of Christ would occur in their own generation, not at a much later date following a thousand-year glory era.

Edwards went into a detailed refutation of this doctrine, now taken as axiomatic by naturalistic critics. In a nineteen-point argument he showed that the apostles, and Christ, taught no such doctrine.[27]

1. The "we" (1 Thess. 4:15f.) does not necessarily refer to that generation (literally understood) but to "dead Christians, who will not be left behind when Christ returns."

2. Uncertainty about the time of Christ's return is seen in the reference to his coming "as a thief in the night."

3. Genesis 50:25 has Joseph foretelling that "God will surely visit you" (not meaning that generation of Jews) "and ye shall carry up my bones from hence."

4. That Paul did not mean that his generation would be alive at the Second Coming is clear in 2 Thessalonians 2:1-3.

5. There is no evidence of a change in Paul's mind, because 2 Thessalonians was written shortly after 1 Thessalonians and while he was still at Athens.

6. First Corinthians 6:14 says that Christ "will raise up us" implying "our" death.

7. Second Thessalonians is so clear and pointed that statements elsewhere must be seen in its light.

8. We must take expectancy passages in this light (that Christ's coming meant the salvation of the church, not that the return would be in their time).

9. Biblical "at hand" did not necessarily mean "at that specific time" as is seen by Haggai 2:6, 7, Malachi 3:1, Isaiah 39:17, 18, and Revelation 1:3.

10. Peter's "thousand years is as a day" did not disappoint the saints, because they knew that Christ would come for them at death.

11. First Corinthians 10:11 shows that many things in the Old Testament times were done for examples centuries later in New Testament times.

12. First Peter 4:7: "The end of all things is at hand." The explanation for this is given in 2 Peter 3:7, 8: The heavens and earth are being kept in store for the appointed time.

13. John 21:22 shows that Christ did not say that he would return before John's death.

14. Revelation 3:11, 12, and 20 seem to expect Christ to come quickly, but the following seventeen chapters show the successive ages that will occur before Christ returns.

15. The church grew strong rather than weak when Christ did not return, showing that Christians were not disillusioned but prepared.

16. Matthew 25:5 says the "bridegroom" (Christ) "tarried."

17. Luke 17:22 and 18:8 show that when Christ speaks of his coming the reference is to special providence: the fall of Jerusalem (cf. 17:37; 19:13-15). The apostles asked about the "time of his coming" and Christ referred to the fall of Jerusalem. When Christ referred to the end of the world it is associated with final judgment, which was not to follow the fall of Jerusalem. After that, the Jewish dispersion and time of the Gentiles were to occur.

18. "In that generation" refers to the fall of Jerusalem (A.D. 70).

19. Christ predicted the calling of Gentiles (Matt. 21:41, 43), which the parables showed would be gradual. He also predicted the dispersal of Jews in all nations (Luke 21:24) before his return.

ELEVEN
HELL

THE NATURE OF HELL

Hell is a spiritual and material furnace of fire where its victims are eternally tortured in their minds and in their bodies by God, the devils, and damned humans, including themselves. Their memories and consciences as well as their raging, unsatisfied lusts torture them. In hell, the place of death, God's saving grace, mercy, and pity are gone forever, never for a moment to return.

Figuratively speaking, the wrath of God is a consuming fire. Dives, in torment spiritually even before the resurrection of his body, was described as existing in fire, begging to have Lazarus wet his tongue to relieve the pain (Luke 16). The metaphor points to the all-over prevalence of the anguish and its intolerable severity. Divine wrath will be far more terrible than its symbol.

But the symbol is also "very probably" literal. Actually, the furnace is figurative so far as the soul is concerned, literal as it pertains to the body. There is nothing impossible about its being literal, and Christ's words in Matthew 10:28 require it.[1] After all, it takes real fire to burn the heavens and earth in the great conflagration, which is hell.

"God will be the hell of one and the heaven of the other."[2]

It is because God is the fire which burns in hell that words can never convey— much less exaggerate— the terrors of the damned. "Who can know the power of his anger?" asked the psalmist (Ps. 90:11). Edwards took this to be a rhetorical question. "The law and the gospel both," he insisted, "agree that God intends an extra-ordinary manifestation of his terribleness."[3] If this be so, it was inevitable that Edwards would assuredly advise: "Let not the sinner imagine that these things are bugbears."[4] Future punishment is contrary neither to Scripture nor reason. In fact, it is most reasonable to suppose it.[5] He gives five arguments to prove that ministers have not set it out "beyond what it really is."[6] He then concludes confidently: "If I therefore have described this misery beyond the truth, then the Scriptures have done the same."[7]

THE LOCALITY OF HELL

"Immediately upon the finishing the judgment and the pronouncing that sentence will come the end of the world. Then the frame of this world shall be dissolved. The pronouncing of that sentence will probably be followed with amazing thunders that shall rend the heaven and shake the earth out of its place. 2 Peter 3:10. . . . Then shall the sea and the waves roar and the rocks shall be thrown down and there shall be an universal wreck of this frame of the world."[8] " 'Tis probably that this earth after the conflagration shall be the place of the damned" (Miscellany 275).

THE DEGREES OF TORMENT

The definitive treatment on degrees of punishment is found in the sermon on Matthew 5:22, "That the punishment and misery of wicked men in another world will be in proportion to the sin that they are guilty of."[9] All men partake "equally" of original sin but men do not partake "equally" of "actual sins."[10] The score is proportionately increased in God's "debt book," although "he that commits one act of sin" (profanity, a breaking of the Sabbath, an intemperate act, etc.) "deserves capital punishment."[11] He has merited only by one sinful act the eternal ruin of soul and body.[12] By a second act—assuming it was no worse—"he now deserves twice so hot a place in hell fire."[13] The "second act of drunkenness . . . heats hell a great deal more than the first." Heinousness of sins is next described and weighed, aggravations considered, and finally the influence or prestige of the sinner put into the balance.[14] Consequently, "The damned in hell would be ready to give the world if they could to have the number of their sins to have been one less."[15]

HELL BEHOLDING THIS WORLD

The parable of Dives and Lazarus, though not to be taken literally ("we need not suppose that there ever was actually such a conversation"), justifies the doctrine that hell remembers this world.[16] The lost "remember what good things they enjoyed here in this world."[17] While they enjoyed the good things, they "felt nothing of the fiery wrath of God."[18] Now it is the reverse. They will remember the "bottle of liquor," "friends," "comfortable habitation," and how they were "a great deal better off than many of the godly."[19] Of particular poignancy will be their recollection of "opportunities" and means they had for obtaining salvation when "God waited to be gracious unto them."[20] They will remember how they were warned "that if once they got into hell they should never get out."[21] Especially, they will remember their sins, including the sin of thinking that hell was a mere "dream."[22]

At the day of judgment "the wicked shall see others glorified."[23] They will see them mount up to meet the Lord in the air, be received, seated at his right hand, and crowned. "Those things will be transacted most publicly in open sight of all wicked men."[24] The lost will see the redeemed "floating to Christ from every region of the earth" — among them those whom the wicked had despised in this world.[25] Hell's sight of the blessedness of heaven will increase the hellishness of hell.

THE ETERNALITY OF HELL

Edwards annihilates the belief in total annihilation. The wicked in the world to come will beg for annihilation, but, Edwards says, it will not occur. He destroys the teaching with a battery of arguments. First, the Bible teaches eternal punishment. It is eternal, for the very word used for eternal life is used for eternal death. This punishment implies pain, which annihilation is not. Annihilation is the relief which the wicked, begging for, will never receive. As the sermon on Revelation 6:15, 16 poignantly described, "Wicked men will hereafter earnestly wish to be turned to nothing and forever cease to be that they may escape the wrath of God."[26] Second, it is also clear that the wicked "shall be sensible of the punishment they are under."[27] Third, degrees of punishment preclude annihilation.[28] Fourth, "The Scripture is very express and abundant in this matter that the eternal punishment is in sensible misery and torment and not annihilation."[29] Furthermore, annihilation is no state at all and is therefore inconsistent with man's soul, which is never destroyed.[30] Sixth, men would never know their judgment if annihilation were their punishment. Instead of God repaying them face to face they would never have to face God at all.[31] But, in the seventh place, wicked men are still alive in hell now, fearing the resurrection of their bodies, as the devils are now dreading the further punishment which is awaiting them. Again, it could not be said that it was better for the wicked not to have been born if they have no judgment awaiting them.[32] In fact, the righteous generally suffer more in this world than the wicked, which would make the latter's annihilation unfair. Ninth, what is the meaning of a burning furnace heated to different degrees if none were ever to be cast into it?[33] Moreover, if the judgment of God begins in the house of God it surely will not spare the unrighteous, and if it was done in a green tree (the innocent Christ), what will happen to the dry? Finally, how could Christ have had to die for us when no punishment threatened?[34]

" 'Tis the infinite almighty God himself that shall become the fire of the furnace exerting his infinite perfections that way."[35] Hell, for Edwards, will not be the absence of God but his presence — his inescapable, wrathful presence. Impenitent sinners will see God face to face forever. That is their hell.

TWELVE
HEAVEN

A chapter on hell should not serve as the conclusion to a study of a man whose life and thought were fixed on the love of God. Edwards, like all scriptural theologians of his own day and ours, believed in the reality of hell, for he believed that terror must inevitably be the lot of those who reject God's offer of forgiveness and love. It is unfair to assume, however, that hell was the center of his message. He did preach the famous sermon "Sinners in the Hands of an Angry God" to a receptive congregation at Enfield, Connecticut, in 1741, but he also preached dozens of sermons on the sweetness of the Christian life. A sermon on Isaiah 32:2 bears the title "Safety, Fulness, and Sweet Refreshment to Be Found in Christ," and in a sense this is more typical of his preaching than the notorious Enfield sermon.

Edwards did preach hellfire sermons. He also wrote lyrically beautiful expressions of his appreciation of nature, and he saw no contradiction in doing both. The God who created the world with all its beauty was also the God of perfect holiness, and a holy God must punish sin. The man who enjoyed horseback rides in the Massachusetts countryside believed that the beauty of the earth was made for man's enjoyment. To enjoy and to ignore the giver of the gift was, to

Edwards, a horrible thing. Life must, he thought, be lived with constant reference to the sovereign God who requires faith and repentance from his human creatures. He himself lived such a life, and the theological works he left to us reveal that the man's thoughts and deeds did not contradict each other.

"Let it be considered that if our lives ben't a journey to heaven they will be a journey to hell."[1] For Jonathan Edwards, there were only two permanent abodes for men and angels. Edwards never tired of describing, proving, demonstrating, and preaching endless heaven and endless hell. But there can be no doubt where his heart was. Even as he defended "the justice of God in the damnation of sinners," he triumphantly extolled the divine and everlasting mercy in the salvation of saints. Jonathan Edwards was in his truest element not as the faithful, fiery preacher of "Sinners in the Hands of an Angry God" — though this he ever was and ever remained — but as the rhapsodic seer of the "beatific vision."[2]

THE NATURE OF HEAVEN

For Edwards, heaven was a manifest implication of the atonement. "He whose arms are opened to suffer to be nailed to the cross will doubtless be opened as wide to embrace those for whom he suffered."

Heaven is where Christ is. The communion of the God-man is that of which they shall eat and drink abundantly,[3] "and swim in the ocean of love, and be eternally swallowed up in the infinitely bright, and infinitely mild and sweet beams of divine love; eternally receiving the light, eternally full of it, and eternally compassed round with it, and everlastingly reflecting it back again to its fountain."[4]

Wonderful as is the fellowship of the saints with their God

and Savior, this does not exclude their delight in one another. "There is no reason to think, that the friendships con-
tracted here on earth between saints that have been
sanctified, by the love of God will be rooted out in another
world."[5] So, saints will recognize fellow saints in heaven and
their love for each other will be perfected.

THE LOCALITY OF HEAVEN

"Heaven is everywhere in Scripture represented as the
throne of God, and that part of the universe, that is God's
fixed abode, and dwelling-place, and that is everlastingly ap-
propriated in that use."[6] There are many places where God
has manifested himself from time to time, but his fixed
abode of manifestation is called heaven, and heaven it
remains.[7]

THE DEGREES OF BLESSEDNESS

"The saints are like so many vessels of different sizes cast into
a sea of happiness where every vessel is full: this is eternal life,
for a man ever to have his capacity filled."[8] This was Edwards' way of explaining Paul's metaphor of the stars of
differing brilliance shining in the same heaven (1 Cor. 15:40,
41).

What determines these differing capacities? It was not the
Atonement, which had the same saving efficacy for all saints.
The varying "sizes" of these perfectly filled vessels were determined by God's "sovereign pleasure." "But after all 'tis left to
God's sovereign pleasure, 'tis his prerogative to determine
the largeness of the vessel. . . . Christ's death and righteousness meddled not with this but left it in God's prerogative . . ." (Miscellany 367).

Nevertheless, in Miscellany 367 Edwards clearly teaches

that the different rewards of the saints in the world to come are related to their works in this world. Are their good works, then, only arbitrary determinations of "God's sovereign pleasure"? The answer is that these "good works" are not strictly good at all in themselves; it is only the sovereign pleasure of God to regard them as such and reward them accordingly, not meritoriously. "Though it be true that the saints are rewarded for their good works, yet it is for Christ's sake only, and not for the excellency of their works in themselves considered, or beheld separately from Christ; for so they have no excellency in God's sight."[9]

GROWTH IN BLESSEDNESS

While the proper time for rewards is not until the end of the world, the saints will "have glorious rewards in heaven immediately after death."[10] The rewards continue in the form of ever-new discoveries of one another, in contrast to this life. He speaks of this in Miscellany 755: "How soon do earthly lovers come to an end of their discoveries of each other's beauty; how soon do they see all that is to be seen!" But in heaven there is "eternal progress" with new beauties always being discovered.

HEAVEN BEHOLDING THIS WORLD

The saints in heaven will be under advantages to see much more of the church than the saints on earth do. The saints in heaven will be in every way more directly and perfectly acquainted with all that appertains to the church and that manifests its glory, the glory of God's wisdom. The blessed fruit and end of the church in the eternal glory, and blessedness of the subjects of the work of God at that day, will be daily in the heavenly saints' view in those that come out of dying bodies to heaven. And according to Miscellany 198, the church in heaven will be much more concerned in it, than one part of the church on earth shall be in the prosperity of another.

HEAVEN BEHOLDING HELL

The Scriptures "plainly teach" that heaven will behold hell just as Lazarus and Abraham saw Dives in his misery (Luke 16:19-31). Isaiah 66:24 is submitted as evidence of heaven beholding hell: "And they shall go forth and look on the carcasses of the men that have transgressed against me: for their worm shall not die, neither shall their fire be quenched." Christ had taught that the sheep on his right hand at the Last Judgment would see the wicked on his left hand and hear Christ say: "Depart from me, ye cursed, into everlasting fire, prepared for the devil and his angels" (Matt. 25:41). So the saints in heaven and sinners in hell shall some way or other have a direct and immediate apprehension of each other's state (Miscellany 1061).

An objection arises: If saints are to grieve now when men go to hell, how can they rejoice then?[11] Edwards gives five answers. First, it is the Christian's duty now to love even the wicked, not knowing but that they may be loved of God. In hell they are seen to be hated of God and so are hated by the saints.[12] Second, all men are now capable of salvation through the efforts of men, but in hell salvation is past forever.[13] Third, rejoicing at calamities may now be because of envy and other evil dispositions, but in heaven saints rejoice only in the glory of God.[14] Fourth, natural affection "is no virtue in the saints in glory. Their virtue will exercise itself in a higher manner."[15] Fifth, when God takes vengeance on oppressors it is always because of his love to his saints.[16] So in hell this infinite love for his own will be be eternally visible

in the punishment of their wicked enemies whom they may
have loved in this world.

THE ETERNALITY OF HEAVEN

That the eternity of the future state of happiness or misery
spoken of in Scripture is a proper eternity, "absolutely ex-
cluding any end, is most clearly manifest by Luke
20:36 . . . and other places."[17] Many more texts are cited to
prove the same point, with the main emphasis on the eter-
nality of heaven proven by the "last enemy," death, being conquered. Not only is heaven eternal, but also "the heavenly
inhabitants do as it were remain in eternal youth."[18]

THE BEATIFIC VISION

Glorious as is the fellowship of the saints with Christ and
other saints and angels, the peak of heavenly blessedness is
the sight of God himself, the *amor intellectualis Dei* (the intellectual love of God). To this supreme theme Edwards gives
intense reflection. "It is no sight of any thing with the bodily
eyes; but it is an intellectual view. The beatifical vision of
God is not a sight with the eyes of the body, but with the eyes
of the soul. There is no such thing as seeing God properly
with the bodily eyes because he is a spirit: one of his attributes is, that he is invisible" (Miscellany 1004).

Not only is the beatific vision not to be physical, Edwards
cannot grant that it can even come about through the senses.
Any earthly empiricism seems to be transcended. "This
highest blessedness of the soul does not enter in at the door
of the bodily senses; this would be to make the blessedness of
the soul dependent on the body, or the happiness of man's
superior part to be dependent on the inferior."[19]

How is this pure idealism proven? The beatific vision of

God is not any sight with the bodily eyes, "because the separate souls of the saints, and the angels which are mere spirits, and never were united to body, have this vision. . . ." Hence, the grand conclusion: " 'Tis not in beholding any form of visible representation, or shape, or colour, or shining light, that the highest happiness of the soul consists in; but 'tis in seeing God, who is a spirit, spiritually, with the eyes of the soul."[20]

"The saints in heaven shall see God."[21]

APPENDIX

CHRONOLOGY OF JONATHAN EDWARDS' LIFE

1703	Born at East Windsor, Connecticut.
1715	Writes "Of Insects."
1716	Enters Yale College.
1720–22	Studies theology in New Haven.
1722	Serves as pastor of a New York Presbyterian church.
1724	Elected to office of tutor at Yale.
1726	Called to Northampton, Massachusetts, church as assistant minister to his grandfather, Solomon Stoddard.
1727	Marries Sarah Pierrepont.
1731	Delivers public lecture at First Church, Boston, titled *God Glorified in Man's Dependence*.
1734	*A Divine and Supernatural Light*. Beginning of Great Awakening in Northampton.
1737	*A Faithful Narrative of the Surprising Work of God*.
1738	*Charity and Its Fruits*.
1739	*Narrative of His Conversion*.
1741	*The Distinguishing Marks of a Work of the Spirit of God*. Preaches "Sinners in the Hands of an Angry God" at Enfield, Connecticut.

1742   *Some Thoughts Concerning the Present Revival of Religion in New England.*

1746   *A Treatise Concerning Religious Affections.*

1747   Death of David Brainerd at the Edwards home.

1748   Beginning of dissension in the Northampton parish.

1750   *Farewell Sermon* delivered at Northampton.

1751   Settles at Stockbridge, Massachusetts, as pastor to the local church and missionary to the Indians.

1754   *A Careful and Strict Enquiry into the Modern Prevailing Notions of Freedom of Will.*

1755   *The Nature of True Virtue* and *The End for Which God Created the World* (both unpublished until 1765).

1757   Chosen president of the College of New Jersey (now Princeton).

1758   Inaugurated president at Princeton. *The Great Christian Doctrine of Original Sin Defended.* Dies of smallpox on March 22.

Left unpublished was the projected work "A Rational Account of the Main Doctrines of the Christian Religion Attempted," which was to be a summation of his Christian philosophy and theology.

The Miscellanies, Edwards' journals and private notes, now fill nine volumes with 1,360 entries, some of them short, some of them elaborate treatises. Edwards gave each entry a title and kept an index. He intended to use the Miscellanies in his "Rational Account." Most of the Miscellanies are not yet fully available in published form.

NOTES

Acknowledgments are made to the Divinity School of Yale University, where the author served as a research fellow. Acknowledgments are also made to the Beinecke Library and Rare Book Room, Yale University, for gracious permission to cite its excellent collection of Edwardsean manuscripts and to its librarians for their courtesy and assistance. The collected *Works* used is that edition edited by Edward Hickman (2 vols., London: William Ball, 1837) unless otherwise noted. Sermon dates prior to 1733 are owing mainly to Thomas A. Schafer, as are many Miscellany quotations, although these are frequently taken from printed works and from the manuscripts directly. The Miscellanies are cited by their numbers or letter. Sermons are indicated by text and doctrine; if they are in print, this is usually indicated. *Notes on the Scriptures* and other works are quoted from the manuscripts and often located, if in print. All manuscripts are quoted in a form as close to the original as feasible for a modern reader. Chapter 2 is heavily indebted to my article "Jonathan Edwards and the Bible," published in *Tenth: An Evangelical Quarterly* (January 1980) and used with that periodical's kind permission. Chapters 11 and 12 are indebted to my *Jonathan Edwards on Heaven and Hell* (Grand Rapids: Baker, 1980).

INTRODUCTION

1. Jan Ridderbos, *De Theologie van Jonathan Edwards* (The Hague: Johan A. Nederbragt, 1907).
2. C. Conrad Cherry, *The Theology of Jonathan Edwards: A Reappraisal* (1966; reprint, Gloucester, Mass.: Peter Smith, 1974).
3. Carl Bogue, *Jonathan Edwards and the Covenant of Grace* (Cherry Hill, N.J.: Mack Publishing, 1975).

4. John H. Gerstner, *Steps to Salvation: The Evangelistic Message of Jonathan Edwards* (Philadelphia: Westminster, 1960).

CHAPTER ONE

1. Vincent Tomas, "The Modernity of Jonathan Edwards," *New England Quarterly* 25 (March 1952): 82.
2. Perry Miller, *Jonathan Edwards* (New York: William Sloan Associates, 1949), cited by John Opie, ed., *Jonathan Edwards and the Enlightenment* (Lexington, Mass.: D. C. Heath, 1969), 33.
3. Clarence H. Faust, "Jonathan Edwards as a Scientist," *American Literature* 1(January 1930): 393-404.
4. Theodore Hornberger, "The Effect of the New Science Upon the Thought of Jonathan Edwards," *American Literature* 9 (November 1937): 190-207.
5. Douglas J. Elwood, *The Philosophical Theology of Jonathan Edwards* (New York: Columbia University Press, 1960).
6. Robert C. Whittemore, "Philosopher of the Sixth Way," *Church History* (March 1966): 60ff.
7. Elwood, *Philosophical Theology,* 51.
8. *Works,* 1:ccxxxiv.
9. Cf. Martin Luther, *The Bondage of the Will,* trans. J. I. Packer and O. R. Johnson (London: J. Clarke, 1957) and Jonathan Edwards, *Freedom of the Will,* ed. Paul Ramsey (New Haven: Yale University Press, 1957).
10. Peter Gay, *A Loss of Mastery: Puritan Historians in Colonial America* (Berkeley: University of California Press, 1966), quoted in Opie, *Edwards and the Enlightenment,* 104f.
11. See John Locke, *The Reasonableness of Christianity and Discourse on Miracles,* ed. I. T. Ramsey (Stanford: Stanford University Press, 1958), 32f., 78ff.
12. Sermon on Romans 2:5, "Unawakened and impenitent sinners do heap up to themselves wrath against the day of wrath as men are wont to heap up treasures," 1731. (Sermon dates given are as accurate as possible. In some cases, we know only the year the sermon was preached. In other cases we may know the exact date and year. Where there is some doubt about a sermon's date, it may be listed in the note with a diagonal—e.g., March 1738/39—indicating that the year was either 1738 or 1739. Or, an inclusive date may be listed—e.g., Spring–Summer 1729—indicating that a specific month or date has not been determined. Some sermons were used on more than one occasion, and this is often indicated in the notes.)
13. *Works,* 2:479.
14. Ibid., 2:479, 480.
15. Ibid., 2:484.

16. Ibid.
17. Ibid., 2:484, 485.

CHAPTER TWO

1. By contrast, Emil Brunner found it essential to begin his theologizing with revelation, as the very title of one of his major works indicates: *Revelation and Reason: The Christian Doctrine of Faith and Knowledge*, trans. Olive Wyon (Philadelphia: Westminster, 1946).
2. Sermon on Romans 3:11.
3. Sermon on Romans 1:20.
4. Sermon on 1 Corinthians 2:11-13.
5. Jonathan Edwards, *A Divine and Supernatural Light* (Boston: S. Kneeland and T. Green, 1734), 15f. We need only remind the reader of other Edwardsean sources, such as *Of Being*, Miscellany 880, and *Freedom of the Will*.
6. Charles Hodge, *Systematic Theology* (New York: Scribner, Armstrong, 1876), 1:49-55.
7. Ibid., 1:49, 50.
8. Ibid., 1:51.
9. Emil Brunner, *The Phiiosophy of Religion from the Standpoint of Protestant Theology*, trans. A. J. P. Farrer and Bartrom Lee Woolf (New York: Scribner's, 1937), 55.
10. *Works*, 2:919.
11. Jonathan Edwards, *The Works of President Edwards, with a Memoir of His Life*, 10 vols., ed. Sereno E. Dwight (New York: S. Converse, 1829), 7:474. Hereafter cited as *Works* (Dwight).
12. Locke, "A Discourse of Miracles," in *Reasonableness of Christianity*, 81.
13. Alexander Grosart, *Selections from the Unpublished Writings of Jonathan Edwards, of America* (printed for private circulation, 1865), 194.
14. Sermon on Luke 16:31: "The warnings of God's word are more fitted to obtain the ends of awakening sinners and bringing them to repentance than the rising of one from the dead to warn them."
15. Notes on Scripture, No. 265. *Works* (Dwight), 8:211, 212.
16. Sermon on Psalm 19:7-10: "The good that is obtained by the word of God lasts forever." Sermon on Matthew 24:35: "God never fails of his word."
17. Grosart, *Selections*, 193.
18. *Works of President Edwards in Four Volumes* (New York: Robert Carter and Brothers, 1879), 3:537. Hereafter cited as *Works* (Carter).
19. *Works* (Dwight), 7:219.
20. *Works* (Carter), 3:538.
21. Cherry, *Theology of Jonathan Edwards*, 47. Cherry himself notes just before this statement that Edwards commonly refers to Scripture

as the Word of God. His discussion throughout these pages detailing the relationship of Word and Spirit is generally sound.

22. W. G. T. Shedd, *Sermons to the Natural Man* (New York: Scribner's, 1871), 285.

23. *Works* (Carter), 3:540.

24. Ibid.

CHAPTER THREE

1. Edwards Amasa Park was probably the first to prove Edwards sound on the Trinity in *Remarks of Jonathan Edwards on the Trinity* (Andover, Mass.: Andover Press, 1881). E. C. Smith's "The Trinity," Appendix I in *Exercises Commemorating the Two-hundredth Anniversary of the Birth of Jonathan Edwards,* October 4 and 5, 1903 (Andover, Mass.: Andover Press, 1904), 7-33, shows that Edwards' thoughts on the Trinity (found in *The Mind* and the Miscellanies) prove him to have been orthodox from the beginning of his intellectual life. George P. Fisher also had printed in 1903 *An Unpublished Essay of Edwards on the Trinity, with Remarks on Edwards and His Theology;* this laid to rest the rumor of Edwards' alleged heresy after detailing its history. It is interesting that Paul Helm has charged Edwards not with unitarianism but with its opposite extreme, tritheism: "What God's idea of himself will be will be not another person of the Godhead but another God . . . implicitly tritheistic," *Treatise on Grace and Other Posthumously Published Writings,* ed. Paul Helm (Cambridge: James Clarke, 1971), 21. This seems a gratuitous criticism, inasmuch as identity of essence does not preclude distinction of person, which Edwards clearly taught.

2. R. A. Delattre, *Beauty and Sensibility in the Thought of Jonathan Edwards* (New Haven: Yale University Press, 1968), 148ff.

3. It was because of the atonement, Edwards says, that the doctrine of the Trinity had been revealed to us *(Works* [Carter], 4:130, 154). One interesting argument for the deity of Christ is that unless he were God, men would be tempted to make him God out of gratitude for the atonement. "God would not have given us any person to be our redeemer, unless he was of divine and absolutely supreme dignity and excellency, or who was the supreme God, lest we should be under temptation to pay him too great respect. . . . Men are very liable to be tempted to rate those too highly from whom they have received great benefits. They are prone to give them that respect and honor that belongs to God only." But it is not possible to honor Christ too much, for he is God and "has done as great things for us as ever the Father did" *(Works* [Carter], 2:509).

4. Jonathan Edwards, *The Mind,* in *Jonathan Edwards' Scientific and*

Philosophical Writings, ed. Wallace E. Anderson (New Haven: Yale University Press, 1980), 337.

CHAPTER FOUR

1. It is interesting to note that in Miscellany 438 Edwards begins, "So it was also with the angels that their judgment was likewise deceived."
2. Jonathan Edwards, *Freedom of the Will,* ed. Paul Ramsey (New Haven: Yale University Press, 1957), 413.

CHAPTER FIVE

1. Sermon on Genesis 3:11, "The act of our first father in eating the forbidden fruit was a very heinous act," February 1738/39.
2. Sermon on Luke 6:35, "God is kind to the unthankful and to the evil, and this appears in his great kindness to mankind who are the subjects of abundance of the kindness and goodness of God and yet are very evil and unthankful," August 1731–December 1732.
3. Sermon on Matthew 10:17, "Children ought to love the Lord Jesus Christ above all things in this world," August 1740.
4. Sermon on Romans 5:10, "Natural men are God's enemies," August 1736.
5. Sermon on Psalm 66:5, "That 'tis to the glory of God that he is terrible in his doings towards the children of men," Spring–Summer 1729.
6. Sermon on Romans 5:10 (see note 4).
7. Sermon on Malachi 1:8, "Men are wont to offer such treatment to God as they will not take one of another," October 1750, April 1752.
8. Sermon on Jeremiah 2:31, "The grand contest between God and sinners is who shall be chief," August 1748.
9. Sermon on Matthew 23:33, " 'Tis in itself most rational to suppose that wicked men should be most extremely and eternally miserable in another world," July 1737.
10. Sermon on Jeremiah 44:4, "Sin is exceeding hateful to God," October 1733, April 1754.
11. Sermon on Habakkuk 1:13, "That God hates sin," before 1733.
12. Sermon on Zechariah 11:8, "There is a mutual loathing and abhorrence between God and wicked men," Fall 1730.
13. Sermon on Luke 19:40, "What is meant is that he (the Son of man) came into the world to seek and save sinners," to the Stockbridge Indians, June 1751. Sermon on Romans 9:18, "God doth exercise his sovereignty in the affair of men's eternal salvation," before 1733.
14. Sermon on Deuteronomy 29:4, "Persons are not at all excused for any moral defect or corruption that is in them, but God doesn't

help them to be otherwise," September 1745.

15. Jonathan Edwards, *Original Sin,* ed. Clyde A. Holbrook (New Haven: Yale University Press, 1970), 183.

16. Ibid., 218.

17. Sermon on Romans 5:7, 8, "There never was any love that could be paralleled with the dying love of Christ," May–June 1731, February 1752.

18. Sermon on Romans 6:14, "That the gospel or new covenant is eminently a dispensation of grace," Spring–Summer 1729.

19. Sermon on Romans 7:14, "That men as they are by nature are perfect slaves to corruption, or they are entirely under the dominion of sin," Winter–Summer 1730.

20. Sermon on Matthew 23:27, "Wicked men's bodies are as it were the sepulchres of their souls," March 1736/37.

21. Sermon on Psalm 139: 23, 24, "Persons should be much concerned to know whether they do not live in some way of sin," September 1733.

22. Two sermons on Matthew 10:17, "That the nature of man is so corrupted that he is become a very evil and hurtful creature," before 1733.

23. Sermon on Luke 17:9, "That God doesn't thank men for doing these things which he commands them," Fall 1727.

24. *Original Sin,* 130.

25. Clyde A. Holbrook thinks that by this line of reasoning Edwards has leveled all sins and inconsistently, therefore, speaks of degrees of heinousness. Nevertheless, he acknowledges that Edwards does justify his inconsistency: "In the Corollary to 'Miscellanies,' No. 713, JE referred to the problem of all sins being equally heinous as 'hardly worth mentioning,' but went on to argue ingeniously that . . . 'some sins may be more aggravated and heinous than others in other respects as if we suppose a cylinder infinitely long can't be greater in that respect . . . yet it may be doubled and trebled, yea, and made a thousandfold more by the increase of other dimensions.' So with sin, it may be vastly more dreadful on other accounts" (*Original Sin,* 11, 12).

26. *Works,* 1:628.

27. Ibid., 1:669.

28. Joseph G. Haroutunian, *Piety Versus Moralism* (New York: Henry Holt, 1932).

29. Sermon on Romans 3:11, 12, "All that natural men do is wrong," April 1736.

30. Four sermons on Ecclesiastes 9:10, "That persons had need to make all possible haste to get that work done that must be done and that

can't be done after death," Spring 1728–Winter 1729; "Persons ought to do what they can for their salvation," December 1733; "Whatever persons look upon needful to be done for their own salvation and intend to do at all, they should do now," January 1733; "What men must do—whatsoever their hand finds to do. Everything that needs to be done in order to their salvation and in order to their being prepared for death," December 1751.

31. Ibid.
32. Ibid.
33. Ibid.
34. Sermon on Matthew 23:15, "Wicked men are the children of hell," January 1738/39.
35. Sermon on Mark 5:16, 17, "The Gadarenes loved their swine better than Jesus Christ," April 1737.
36. *Original Sin,* 132-133.

CHAPTER SIX

1. *Works* (Carter), 3:542.
2. Ibid., 2:565.
3. Ibid., 2:566.
4. Ibid.
5. Ibid., 2:567.
6. Ibid., 2:569.
7. For Edwards, atonement is the sacrifice of Christ. Edwards contrasts this with the typical Old Testament sacrifices in a sermon on Psalm 40:6-8, "That the sacrifice is the only sacrifice that is upon its own account acceptable to God," Summer–Fall 1729. Commenting on the Old Testament anticipations, Edwards poignantly observes that by the "ceremonial law the gospel was preached." Believers are so united to Christ that his sacrifice is theirs.
8. Heinrich Heppe, *Reformed Dogmatics,* trans. G. T. Thomson (London: George Allan and Unwin, 1950), 458-462.
9. Sermon on John 14:27.
10. Sermon on Isaiah 53:10, "Christ in his last sufferings suffered extremely from the hand of God the Father," May 1744.
11. Sermon on Hebrews 9:13, 14.
12. Sermon on Revelation 14:3, "The nature of the redemption of God's elect," November 1741.
13. Sermon on Galatians 2:20, "That Christ had a particular respect to every believer in what he did and suffered in the work of redemption," Spring 1728–Winter 1729.
14. Sermon on Romans 2:10.
15. Ibid.

16. Sermon lecture on Romans 8:29, 30, December 7, 1739.
17. Sermon on Revelation 14:3 (see note 12).
18. Louis Berkhof, *The History of Christian Doctrine* (Grand Rapids: Eerdmans, 1953), 200.
19. See Dorus Paul Rudisill, *The Doctrine of the Atonement in Jonathan Edwards and His Successors* (New York: Poseidon Books, 1971).

CHAPTER SEVEN

1. *Original Sin*, 362.
2. *Works*, 2:553.
3. Ibid., 2:543.
4. Ibid., 2:543f.
5. Ibid., 2:554f.
6. Ibid., 2:549.
7. Ibid., 2:548.
8. Sermon on Ephesians 2:5-7, "When a sinner is converted, 'tis so glorious and blessed a work that it is worthy never to be forgotten but to be celebrated forevermore," December 1734.
9. *Works*, 2:556.
10. Ibid., 2:564.
11. Four sermons on Acts 26:18, November–December 1747.
12. *Works*, 2:562.
13. Cf. the sermon on John 3:8: "God is sovereign in the work of conversion," yet this does not deny that those most desirous of conversion are most likely to obtain it.
14. *Works*, 2:557.
15. Ibid., 2:558.
16. Ibid., 2:559.
17. Two sermons on Romans 7:14, "That men as they are by nature are perfect slaves to corruption or they are entirely under the dominion of sin," Winter–Summer 1730.
18. Two sermons on John 1:47, " 'Tis a great thing to be indeed a converted person," September 1799.
19. Sermon on 1 Thessalonians 5:23, "In true conversion men's bodies are in some respect changed as well as their souls," July 1740.
20. Lecture on Romans 8:29, 30, "The things which God does for the salvation and blessedness of the saints are like an inviolable chain reaching from a duration without beginning to a duration without end," December 1739.
21. Sermon on Matthew 15:26, "There is a great difference between converted and unconverted men," Summer–Fall 1729.
22. Cf. Helm, *Treatise on Grace*.
23. *Works*, 2:551.

24. Ibid., 2:544, 553.
25. Ibid., 2:561.
26. Ibid., 2:557, 558.
27. Ibid., 2:562.
28. Ibid.
29. Ibid., 2:550.
30. Ibid., 2:543.
31. Ibid., 2:561
32. Ibid., 2:543.
33. Ibid., 2:544.
34. Ibid., 2:543.
35. Ibid.
36. Ibid., 2:544.
37. Ibid., 2:562.
38. Ibid., 2:555.
39. Ibid., 2:558, 559.
40. Ibid., 2:553.
41. Ibid., 2:554
42. Ibid., 2:551.
43. Ibid., 2:553.
44. Ibid., 2:543.
45. Ibid., 2:565.
46. Ibid., 2:551, 552.
47. Ibid., 2:551, 558, 562.

CHAPTER EIGHT

1. Berkhof, *History of Doctrine*, 207.
2. Ibid.
3. Ibid., 211. Berkhof does grant that "in some passages he [Edwards] evidently rises to a higher conception."
4. Whitney Oates, ed., *The Basic Writings of St. Augustine* (New York: Random House, 1968), 2:142.
5. Ibid., 2:215.
6. Ibid., 2:286.
7. Ibid., 2:826.
8. P. Bergauer, *Der Jakobusbrief bei Augustinus* (Freiburg, Germany: Herder, Wren, 1962).
9. Ian Sellers, "Justification," in *The New International Dictionary of the Christian Church*, ed. J. D. Douglas (Grand Rapids: Zondervan, 1978), 557.
10. A. H. Strong, *Systematic Theology* (Old Tappan, N.J.: Fleming H. Revell, 1907), 849.

11. Berkhof, *History of Doctrine*, 225.
12. Edward Boehl, *Justification*, trans. C. H. Riedesel (Grand Rapids: Eerdmans, 1946), 59.
13. Christopher Fitzsimmons Allison, *The Rise of Moralism* (New York: Seabury, 1966).
14. Quoted in Allison, *Rise of Moralism*, 157.
15. Charles Hodge, *Systematic Theology* (Greenwood, S.C.: The Attic Press, 1960), 3:133f.
16. Allison, *Rise of Moralism*, 177.
17. Strong, *Systematic Theology*, 864.
18. *Works* (Carter), 4:177.
19. Ibid., 4:64-132. First published in *Discourses on Various Important Subjects* (Boston: S. Kneeland and T. Green, 1738).
20. Contribution Lecture, December 7, 1739.
21. *Works* (Carter), 4:64-132.
22. See Miscellanies 797 and 829 and sermons on Romans 5:17 and Galatians 4:4, 5.
23. Sermon on Romans 4:16, probably between winter and summer 1730.
24. Ibid.
25. *Works* (Carter), 4:371.
26. Ibid.
27. Ibid.
28. Sermon preached before 1733.
29. Gerstner, *Steps to Salvation*, 76, 77.
30. *Works* (Carter), 4:66. In this connection Edwards cites 1 Peter 3:18 and 1 Timothy 3:16 in support of his contention.
31. Ibid., 4:69.
32. Ibid., 2:517.
33. Ibid., 4:73.
34. Ibid.
35. Sermon on Romans 4:16 (see note 23).
36. Ibid.
37. Ibid.
38. Quoted in Gerstner, *Steps to Salvation*, 146.
39. Cherry, *Theology of Jonathan Edwards*, 203.
40. Outline sermon delivered at Nathan Phelps' home, December 1743, later in 1753 at Stockbridge. Holdings of Andover Divinity School.
41. Sermon preached before 1733.
42. Thomas A. Schafer, "Jonathan Edwards' Conception of the Church," *Church History*, Vol. 24, No. 1 (March 1955).
43. *Freedom of the Will*, 431-437.

44. Ibid., 275-333.
45. Sermon on Romans 4:5.
46. *Works* (Carter), 4:124.
47. Ibid., 4:116.

CHAPTER NINE

1. William Haller, *The Rise of Puritanism* (New York: Harper, 1957), 141. Sibbes's *The Bruised Reed* was perhaps the most effective statement that any preacher accomplished of the "dynamic element in the Puritan morality" (p. 160).
2. Richard Sibbes, *The Bruised Reed*, 5th ed. (London, 1635), 62. He continues, "Those are misled that make Christ to be only righteousness to us, except by imputation, whereas it is a great part of our happiness to be under such a Lord" (p. 79).
3. A. V. G. Allen, *Jonathan Edwards* (Boston: Houghton Mifflin, 1890), 59.
4. Sermon on Micah 3:11, "A pretense of trusting in Christ is a vain pretense as long as men live wicked lives," before 1733.
5. Sermon on John 1:16, "That believers do receive of Christ, of the benediction he himself hath, and do partake with him therein," before 1733, June 1752.
6. Sermon on Matthew 7:21, "That not everyone that saith unto Christ, 'Lord, Lord,' shall enter into the kingdom of heaven," before 1733.
7. Sermons on Hebrews 12:14, "None will ever be admitted to see Christ but only holy persons," August 1731–December 1732.
8. Sermon on Isaiah 35:8, "Those only that are holy are in the way to heaven," Fall 1722–Spring 1723.
9. Ibid.
10. Ibid.
11. Sermon on Luke 6:35, "God is kind to the unthankful and to the evil, and this appears in his great kindness to mankind who are the subjects of abundance of the kindness and goodness of God and yet are very evil and unthankful," before 1733.
12. Sermon on Isaiah 35:8 (see note 8).
13. Sermon on Psalm 119:3, "The spirit that godly men are of is a spirit to be perfectly holy," May 1737, January 1757.
14. Sermon on Job 2:3, "When the professors of religion walk according to their profession, God is so exalted by it that he thereby obtains a glorious triumph over the devil," October 1744.
15. Sermon on James 2:18, "A manifesting of godliness in a man's life and walk is a better ground of others' charity concerning his godli-

ness than any account that he give about it in words," May 1736.

16. *Works* (Carter), 4:332-416.

17. Sermon on Psalm 119:3, May 1737.

18. Sermon on Psalm 139:23, 24, "Persons should be much concerned to know whether they do not live in some way of sin," September 1733.

19. Sermon on Luke 10:42, "That grace is the one thing needful. True grace is the good part. 'Tis called the good part by way of eminency as being incomparably the best part," before 1733.

20. Sermon on Matthew 7:21.

21. Ibid.

22. Sermon on 2 Timothy 3:5, "True grace in the heart is a powerful thing," June 1737.

23. Sermon on Matthew 5:27, 28, "The law of God is exceedingly strict," April 1733.

24. Sermon on Proverbs 17:27, "That the spirit of true godliness is an excellent spirit," before 1733.

25. Sermon on 2 Corinthians 15:1, 2, "The way for those that have the presence of God not to lose it is to take heed of themselves as to these two things: that they don't forsake him and that they still seek him," April 1742.

26. Sermon on Galatians 5:17, September 1745.

27. Sermon on Matthew 7:21 (see note 6).

28. Sermon on Ephesians 6:11-13, July 1744, November 1755.

29. Two Sermons on Luke 22:32, August 1740.

30. Sermon on Revelation 17:14, "Those that are Christ's and belonging to him, 'tis of God that they are so. They that belong to Jesus Christ, they are faithful to Christ," before 1733.

31. Sermon on Luke 7:35, July 1747.

32. Sermon on Matthew 12:7, "Moral duties toward men are a more important and essential part of religion than external acts of worship of God," January 1739/40.

33. Sermon on Matthew 11:29, "They that do truly come to Christ at the same time take Christ's yoke upon them," before 1733.

34. Sermon on Acts 19:19, "When the Spirit of God has been remarkably poured out on a people, a thorough reformation of those things that before were amiss amongst them ought to be the effect of it," April 1736.

35. Ibid.

36. Sermon on Matthew 22:14, to the Stockbridge Indians, April 1755.

37. *Works* (Dwight), 6:214.

38. Sermon on Matthew 7:13, 14, at a private meeting, June 1740/41.

CHAPTER TEN

1. Sermon on Ecclesiastes 11:2, "We ought to prepare for whatever changes may come to pass." December 11, 1737 (after an earthquake on December 7).
2. Sermon on Isaiah 26:10, 11, September 1740.
3. Sermon on Matthew 24:35, "That God never fails of his word," Winter–Spring 1727.
4. Sermon on 2 Chronicles 20:20-29, "When any of God's people have been forth to war and God has remarkably appeared to fight for them and return them to the people and house of God in prosperity, it is an occasion that requires much praise and thanksgiving to God."
5. Sermon on John 1:10.
6. Sermon on Isaiah 27:13, June 1741.
7. Ibid.
8. Sermon on Isaiah 62:6, April 1741.
9. Sermon on Isaiah 41:19, "In the future glorious times of the church of God in this world, the saints shall be like trees that are always green," June 1742.
10. *Works,* 2:31.
11. Sermon on Ecclesiastes 11:2 (see note 1).
12. Ibid.
13. Jonathan Edwards, *Apocalyptic Writings,* ed. Stephen J. Stein (New Haven: Yale University Press, 1977), 342-343.
14. Ibid., 166.
15. Ibid., 178f.
16. *Works,* 2:31.
17. Ibid., 1:384, 385.
18. Note on 1 Corinthians 15:24 in Edwards' blank Bible.
19. H. Richard Niebuhr, *The Kingdom of God in America* (Chicago: Willett, Clark, 1937).
20. *Works,* 2:800.
21. Miscellany 867, in *The Philosophy of Jonathan Edwards from His Private Notebooks,* ed. Harvey G. Townsend (Eugene, Ore.: University of Oregon Press, 1955), 263.
22. Sermon on John 1:10, 11, "Christ came to world and church by his Spirit and his human presence," July 1741.
23. Ibid.
24. Sermon on Hebrews 9:28, March 1749/50.
25. Sermon on 2 Timothy 4:8, May 1752, June 1752.
26. Sermon on John 1:10, 11 (see note 22).
27. *Works,* 2:466f.

CHAPTER ELEVEN

1. Sermon on Matthew 10:28, "That the bodies of wicked men as well as their souls will be punished forever in hell." Winter–Spring 1728.
2. Ibid.
3. Sermon on Job 41:9, 10, "We may in some measure judge how much more terrible the fierceness of God's wrath is than that of creatures by the difference there is between him and them," January 1742/43.
4. Ibid.
5. Ibid.
6. *Works,* 2:884.
7. Ibid., 2:885.
8. Sermon on Romans 2:8, 9.
9. Sermon on Matthew 5:22, Fall 1727.
10. Ibid.
11. Ibid.
12. Ibid.
13. Ibid.
14. Ibid.
15. Ibid.
16. Two sermons on Luke 16:25, "The wicked in hell will remember how things were here in this world. The wicked in hell will be sensible what a happy state the saints are in heaven," before 1733.
17. Ibid.
18. Ibid.
19. Ibid.
20. Ibid.
21. Ibid.
22. Ibid.
23. Sermon on Luke 16:28, "Wicked men will hereafter have this to aggravate their woe, that they see many of all kinds and nations admitted into glory when they themselves are thrust out," to the Stockbridge Indians.
24. Ibid.
25. Ibid.
26. Sermon on Revelation 6:15, 16, August 1731, December 1732, October 1755.
27. Sermon on Matthew 25:46, April 1739.
28. Ibid.
29. Ibid.
30. Ibid.
31. Ibid.
32. Ibid.

33. Ibid.
34. Ibid.
35. Ibid.

CHAPTER TWELVE

1. Sermon on Hebrews 11:13, 14, "This life ought to be spent by us as to be only a journey towards heaven," September 1733. *Works,* 2:243f.
2. John H. Gerstner, *Jonathan Edwards on Heaven and Hell* (Grand Rapids: Baker, 1980), 93. Quotations in this chapter are taken from this book, except as otherwise noted.
3. Sermon on Luke 22:20, "The saints shall hereafter as it were eat and drink with Christ at his table in his Kingdom of Glory."
4. Sermon on 2 Corinthians 5:8. *Works,* 2:29.
5. Sermon on Romans 2:10.
6. The Farewell Sermon (1750) envisages the saints of Northampton meeting their ejected pastor (Edwards) for the final adjudication of the affair. Edwards does not anticipate the verdict of the court, but he assumes that either pastor or people would be vindicated. Would the loser be ejected from heaven or gladly acknowledge his error and enjoy perfect fellowship forevermore? Edwards does not say, but we would infer from his view of heaven that the false saints would be ejected (though not solely because of that one error) and the true ones eternally forgiven and reconciled.
7. *Works,* 2:630.
8. Ibid.
9. Ibid., 2:643f.
10. Ibid., 2:644.
11. Ibid., 2:209, 210.
12. Ibid., 2:210.
13. Ibid.
14. Ibid.
15. Ibid.
16. Ibid.
17. Ibid.
18. Ibid.
19. Quarterly lecture, November 1747.
20. *Works,* 2:900.
21. Ibid.